The Flint Water Crisis:

Systemic Racism Through the Lens of Flint

Report of the

Michigan Civil Rights Commission

February 17, 2017

Special Thank You:

The Michigan Civil Rights Commission wishes to acknowledge the tireless efforts of Dan Levy, MDCR Director of Law & Policy, in researching and drafting this report; Colleen Pero, MDCR Deputy Director for serving as an editor and sounding board; and to Shawn Sanford, Executive Assistant to the Director, who provided the necessary administrative and logistical support to make the Hearings a success.

And a special thank you to MDCR Executive Director Agustin Arbulu not only for his drafting efforts and enthusiasm for the subject matter, but for his steadfast leadership and oversight throughout the Hearing process.

February 17, 2017

Dear Reader,

On January 25, 2016, the Michigan Civil Rights Commission unanimously passed a resolution to hold a series of hearings to determine if any civil rights had been abridged by the contamination of the Flint water distribution system.

At all three hearings, we heard of the many challenges and hardships faced by residents unable to access clean drinking water. We also toured several Flint neighborhoods, meeting with residents and hearing how their lives had been affected and changed immeasurably. The July 14th and September 8th hearings included expert testimony focusing on the history of Flint's economy and housing, environmental justice, and the application of the current emergency manager law.

Reviewing the historical governmental actions impacting the living and health conditions of Flint residents, i.e., the legacy of Flint, was sobering and left a deep impression. We must come to terms with the ongoing effects of "systemic racism" that repeatedly led to disparate racial outcomes as exemplified by the Flint Water Crisis. This can no longer be ignored.

We also offer recommendations intended to ensure that "another Flint" does not happen again – in Flint or anywhere in Michigan. We urge those with authority to carefully consider and act upon these recommendations.

On behalf of the Michigan Civil Rights Commission and Michigan Department of Civil Rights, we wish to thank everyone who testified and submitted written testimony, as well as those who provided additional insight and information for inclusion in this report.

Sincerely,

Michigan Civil Rights Commission

Rasha Demashkieh, Co-Chair   Laura Reyes Kopack JD, Co-Chair
Mumtaz Haque   Arthur M. Horwitz
Deloris Hunt   Ricardo Resio
Linda Lee Tarver   Bradley Voss

February 17, 2017

Dear People of Flint,

The Michigan Civil Rights Commission voted unanimously on January 25, 2016 to hold a series of at least three public hearings to gather testimony to determine if any actions resulting in the poisoning of Flint's public water supply abridged your civil rights under state law.

At the time of its first hearing in Flint on April 28, 2016, various investigations were in progress by local, state and national authorities focusing mostly on assigning blame for actions taken - or not taken - by public officials, and assessing the short- and long-term health and economic impact on you, your children, and your community.

The Michigan Civil Rights Commission decided not to replicate these investigations. Rather, through your sworn testimony, those of subject experts and field visits, we sought to better understand the role decades of structural and institutional discrimination and racism played in quieting your voices and enabling the poisoning of your public water supply.

The immediate needs of the people of Flint, including the provision of bottled water and filters, the deployment of school nurses, and tending to the special needs of children and the elderly, were being addressed by a variety of state and local agencies. However, not everyone knew these goods and services were available. The Michigan Civil Rights Commission and the Michigan Department of Civil Rights, sought to ensure these efforts were communicated and available to all Flint residents, regardless of race, religion, language spoken, disability, country of origin or legal status.

During the course of our Flint hearings, which in addition to April 28th, were held on July 14th and September 8th, many of you told us on the record and privately that you had lost "trust" in government at all levels. However, you also told us that based on how it conducted itself in Flint, the Michigan Civil Rights Commission offered your last hope for obtaining a measure of justice and respect.

A major focus of our report is to present recommendations intended to ensure that "another Flint" does not happen again – in Flint or anywhere in Michigan. While the scope of our hearings and report are framed by state law, you will notice we reference the 2015 U.S. Supreme Court decision, *Texas Department of Housing & Community Affairs v. The Inclusive Communities Project, Inc,* which may offer an opportunity to explore an additional avenue of potential redress.

In assessing our own actions in the months leading up to the Flint Water Crisis, the Michigan Civil Rights Commission and the Michigan Department of Civil Rights acknowledge that we were not as proactive as we should have been in giving greater voice to your concerns of the tainted water. This was especially important because your voices were ignored by state, state-appointed, and local officials. The Commission and the Department pledge to be more resolute in carrying out their unique role under the state Constitution in the future.

The people of Flint have been subjected to unprecedented harm and hardship, much of it caused by structural and systemic discrimination and racism that have corroded your city, your institutions, and your water pipes, for generations. When the last of the civil lawsuits and attorney general criminal investigations are completed, and relief dollars from state and federal sources are exhausted, what will remain is a city and its people who will continue to fight against built-in barriers but whose voices – as a matter of public right – must never be stifled or quelled again. The Michigan Civil Rights Commission and the Michigan Department of Civil Rights will do their part to proactively engage you, listen to you, advocate for you and defend you, to the fullest extent allowed by the civil rights laws of the State of Michigan.

Sincerely,

Michigan Civil Rights Commission

Rasha Demashkieh, Co-Chair	Laura Reyes Kopack JD, Co-Chair
Mumtaz Haque	Arthur M. Horwitz
Deloris Hunt	Ricardo Resio
Linda Lee Tarver	Bradley Voss

Contents

EXECUTIVE SUMMARY

In January 2016, a series of states of emergency for the City of Flint were declared by the Mayor, the Governor and even the President. These declarations turned the attention of the state and nation to the Flint water crisis. As a result, the state, local and federal governments sprang into action. The National Guard was tasked to assist. FEMA[1] sent representatives. Community organizations and non-profits from throughout the state, and even nationally, responded by volunteering, and sending bottled water. The Governor formed Mission Flint, which brought key members of the Administration together weekly, and the Legislature authorized a supplemental budget. Bottled water and water filters were distributed and residents were provided information in multiple languages. It was all hands on deck. From all accounts, the government was operating the way we would expect it to operate in response to an emergency.

What then, was the problem? The timing. Preceding this flurry of "state of emergency" activity, Flint residents had been reporting heavily discolored and bad tasting water for well over a year.

- *On August 15, and September 5, 2014*, Genesee County issued boil water advisories.
- *October 13, 2014,* GM ceased using the water citing corrosion concerns on its parts.
- *October 14, 2014,* senior staff from the Governor's office urged a return to the Detroit water system.
- *January 12, 2015,* State provided water coolers and bottled waters to its employees in Flint.
- *January 30, 2015,* an increase in legionella was linked to the change in water source.
- *February 25, 2015,* a Flint resident contacted the Environmental Protection Agency (EPA) regarding the extremely high levels of lead in her water.
- *February 26, 2015,* the EPA told water personnel that a corrosion program should be in place.
- *June 24, 2015,* EPA confirms "High Lead Levels in Flint, Michigan."
- *July 22, 2015,* the Governor's chief of staff noted that Flint residents did not believe their complaints were being heard.
- *August 27, 2015,* Virginia Tech Professor Marc Edwards reports finding very high lead levels in water.
- *September 24, 2015,* Dr. Mona Hanna-Attisha of Hurley Hospital finds very high lead levels in children.

---

[1] The Federal Emergency Management Agency.

- ***On September 29, 2015***, the Detroit Free Press published an analysis of the blood tests, Genesee County issued a health advisory, and the Governor's office directed the Department of Health & Human Services (DHHS) and the Department of Environmental Quality (DEQ) to consider emergency responses.
- ***On October 1, 2015***, three months before the states of emergency were issued, DHHS confirmed Dr. Hanna-Attisha's analysis.
- ***On October 16, 2015,*** Flint switched back to Detroit water system.
- ***On October 21, 2015,*** the Governor created the Flint Water Advisory Task Force to review state, federal and municipal actions, and to offer recommendations – one year after the first boil water advisory had been issued and GM said they could no longer use the water because it was corroding their parts.
- ***December 14, 2015,*** Flint emergency declaration.
- ***January 4, 2016,*** Genesee County emergency declaration.
- ***January 5, 2015***, State of Michigan emergency declaration.
- ***January 16, 2016***, U.S. Federal emergency declaration.

The Commission recognizes that there have been numerous articles, hearings, studies, reports and investigations into Flint's water crisis. Many focused on the technical aspects of the water crisis: What anti corrosive materials should have been added? What about the testing of lead in the water? Is the current lead copper rule sufficient? Others examined the decision-making tree: who made what decisions and when, and what were the effects of those decisions? And of course, the Attorney General began his investigation into potential criminal wrong-doing. In each of these investigations, the focus has been on who should bear the blame, especially relating to decisions made and actions taken in the last two to three years. There are also numerous private law suits seeking to find liability and hold parties responsible.

The Michigan Civil Rights Commission (MCRC or Commission) believes that to properly and completely assess the causes of the Flint water crisis, we must look back much further. We believe the underlying issue is historical and systemic, and dates back nearly a century, and has at its foundation race and segregation of the Flint community. These historical policies, practices, laws and norms fostered and perpetuated separation of race, wealth and opportunity.

We are not suggesting that those making decisions related to this crisis were racists, or meant to treat Flint any differently because it is a community primarily made up by people of color. Rather, the disparate response is the result of systemic racism that was built into the foundation and growth of Flint, its industry and the suburban area surrounding it. This is revealed through the story of housing, employment, tax base and regionalization which are interconnected in creating the legacy of Flint.

As we explored our premise, we focused on several major areas: implicit bias, the history of segregated housing and education in Flint, and finally, environmental justice and the emergency manager law and how they interconnected to play significant roles leading to the Flint water crisis.

> "While we almost universally recognize that racial discrimination is wrong, this consensus has not translated into decision-making or policies..."

While we almost universally recognize that racial discrimination is wrong, this consensus has not translated into decision-making or policies that reflect those values. What explains this dichotomy? Implicit bias refers to stereotypes or attitudes that operate without a person's conscious awareness. Research confirms that individuals experience implicit bias against a broad range of groups that is often based on race, ethnicity, nationality, gender or social status. Multiple studies have established that every one of us has implicit biases and stereotypes, and that these biases unconsciously influence our decision-making, and often lead to inappropriate decisions regarding people who fall into these categories.

The City of Flint's long history of segregation in housing and education also plays a role. Historically, Flint's community of color was long relegated to substandard housing, education, and job opportunities. Initially, the segregation was a result of both private discrimination (restrictive covenants) and government policies (mortgage requirements, school district lines, etc.). Of course, much of this was made possible because American jurisprudence at the time was largely based upon the U.S. Supreme Court's adoption of the "separate but equal" doctrine in *Plessy v Fergusson*.[2]

These policies built upon each other to such an extent that, if you were an African American or an immigrant from certain countries, it was almost impossible for you to buy a home outside a few neighborhoods designated for people of color, or to attend a school that wasn't overcrowded, let alone one that would prepare you for college. Even industry was complicit: until the end of WWII, jobs for people of color were limited to janitorial positions or the stifling work within the foundries.

We also examine the systems, structures, policies and processes created during the past century that helped shape racialized outcomes in Flint. As Flint grew, many residents left the city for suburban life, but the remaining government policies and private restrictive covenants kept people of color confined to the same three or four neighborhoods within the city limits. By 1970, government policies had officially changed and the written restrictive covenants were expunged. But the legacy of discrimination remained. It has brought the City of Flint to where

---

[2] *Plessy v. Ferguson*, 163 US 537 (1896), was controlling until reversed by *Brown v. Board of Education of Topeka*, 347 U.S. 483 (1954).

it now finds itself – with a majority of its residents being people of color, and their complaints, along with those of their white neighbors, largely ignored.

This brings us to the question: Would the Flint water crisis have been allowed to happen in Birmingham, Ann Arbor or East Grand Rapids? We believe the answer is no, and that the vestiges of segregation and discrimination found in Flint made it a unique target. The lack of political clout left the residents with nowhere to turn, no way to have their voices heard. This brings us to the final two areas covered by this report: Environmental Justice and the Emergency Manager Law.

Environmental Justice requires that all people and communities receive the equal protection of environmental and public health laws, and should have an equal and meaningful voice in decisions related to their environment. As the Governor's Flint Water Advisory Task Force found, the Flint water crisis is an example of environmental injustice. The people of Flint did not enjoy the equal protection of environmental or public health laws, nor did they have a meaningful voice in the decisions leading up to the Flint Water Crisis. Many argue they had *no* voice.

We believe that if the State of Michigan had an environmental justice plan in place, this crisis could have been mitigated and maybe even prevented. We will never know. Equally, had the emergency manager law focused on the financial health of the city *and* the welfare of its residents, and not just on cost-cutting measures, and/or had it allowed for meaningful involvement of the community when it came to the very basic needs of life, clean water and clean air, this too could have served to mitigate or even prevent the water crisis.

This report is triggered by the Flint Water Crisis, but in many ways is not just about Flint. This report seeks to outline a broader framework to explain why the crisis occurred and to propose a set of recommendations that minimizes and safeguards against similar crises in the future. Our report is not meant to assess blame, but to help ensure that such a crisis does not occur in the future and to address shortcomings that continue to persist over time. Accordingly, we offer recommendations that will lessen the likelihood of such a tragedy in the future. Briefly, we recommend:

1. The Michigan Civil Rights Commission and Department of Civil Rights must do a better job of responding and listening to the constituencies we represent, and of making their priorities our priorities.
   a. The Department will develop a mechanism for Department staff to identify and inform the Commission of instances in which the civil rights of a community or constituency are being ignored or adversely affected.
   b. The Commission will relocate scheduled meetings to affected communities when appropriate.
   c. The Department and Commission will facilitate communication of concerns even when not adopting them as a priority of their own.

2. Develop a deeper understanding of the roles of structural racialization and implicit bias, and how they affect decision-making throughout all branches of state government, and specifically within state departments and agencies. The Governor's office should invite experts on implicit bias to provide training on implicit bias to the Cabinet and Mission Flint, and require all state departments, including DHHS and DEQ, to do the same for their staff.

3. Provide environmental justice to all people in Michigan.
   a. Write and legislatively adopt a robust environmental justice plan that includes the following components:
      i. Meaningful public (community participation)
      ii. Integration of government decision-making,
      iii. Interagency cooperation, and
      iv. A means for the public to request responsive state action, i.e., appeal certain decisions.
   b. Amend the emergency manager law to provide for local representation and the ability to appeal an adverse decision.
   c. Acknowledge the cumulative effect of environmental hazards, and make cumulative effect part of the official decision-making process.
   d. Require a more holistic review of the cost-benefit analysis conducted when assessing and placing potential environmental hazards.

4. Replace or restructure Michigan's emergency manager law.
   a. A law intended to help a community recover from a fiscal emergency must be directed at solving the problem that caused the emergency, and thereby returning the community to sustainable fiscal health.
   b. Provide emergency managers with regional authority; not all solutions are local because not all problems are local.
   c. Bifurcate the process of naming an emergency manager and providing special authority or powers.
   d. A declaration of a fiscal emergency that requires emergency management or other state usurpation of local government powers, must include a statement that analyzes the root cause of the emergency and outlines how it will be addressed.
   e. Locally elected representative government must continue to play some role, and an emergency manager must have direct accountability to an elected official (the Governor).

5. Acknowledge the role race and racism have played in our history, and how it continues to impact our present, in order to adopt policies that consider and address it.

6. Rebuild trust and credibility through the creation of a "Truth and Reconciliation Commission" and the integration of a racial equity framework within state government.

7. Create and implement a form of regional government (or at least regional cooperation) that would require suburbs and the urban cores from which they grew to work collaboratively to solve problems.

> "...was race a factor in the Flint Water Crisis?" Our answer is an unreserved and undeniable -- "yes".

The Commission believes that we have answered our initial question, "was race a factor in the Flint Water Crisis?" Our answer is an unreserved and undeniable -- "yes".

We do not base our finding on any particular event. It is based on a plethora of events and policies that so racialized the structure of public policy that it systemically produced racially disparate outcomes adversely affecting a community that is primarily made up of people of color.

Having answered our initial question, we now ask (but leave unanswered), another: If, without racist intent, a systemic problem repeatedly produces different results based on people's skin color, how long does it take before leaving the system in place is itself racism?

We do not believe it is possible to remedy the past harms caused by racism, or the present harms caused by its legacy, without consciously and deliberately addressing and eradicating them.

I. INTRODUCTION

On January 25, 2016, the Michigan Civil Rights Commission (MCRC or Commission) passed a resolution to hold hearings to review the Flint Water Crisis from a civil rights perspective.[3] This report is based on public testimony and public comment received at the hearings, as well as written testimony and other reports made available to the Michigan Department of Civil Rights (MDCR or Department).

By the time the MCRC met in January of 2016, bottled water, test kits and water filters were being provided to Flint residents. The National Guard had been brought in to assist with distribution. Efforts were underway to replace water pipes and infrastructure. Groups had been formed to examine possible health effects and what could be done to minimize the harm caused.

An official task force was created by the governor,[4] and another created by the legislature,[5] both examining the role played by government agencies. Criminal and civil investigations were launched by the Michigan Attorney General, and there were also separate but parallel federal investigations. The Attorney General's investigations have employed as many 18 lawyers, 12 investigators, and numerous support staff. (The office spent roughly half of the $4.9 million

---

[3] Article 5, Section 29 of the Michigan Constitution and the Elliott-Larsen Civil Rights Act give the Commission the authority to hold hearings to investigate alleged discrimination and to secure equal protection of civil rights without such discrimination.

[4] On October 21, 2015, Governor Rick Snyder created the Flint Water Advisory Task Force. Its March 2016, final report can be found at https://www.michigan.gov/documents/snyder/FWATF_FINAL_REPORT_21March2016_517805_7.pdf (accessed February 10, 2017).

[5] The Joint Select Committee on the Flint Water Emergency was created by Senate Concurrent Resolution 24 of 2016. Its final report, *FLINT WATER CRISIS: An Action Plan for Michigan*, can be found at https://misenategopcdn.s3.amazonaws.com/99/publications/Final%20Report%20of%20the%20Joint%20Select%20Committee.pdf (accessed February 10, 2017).

allocated to it by the Michigan Legislature by October of 2016.)[6] The criminal investigation has to date resulted in criminal charges against nine individuals, and is ongoing.

In addition, numerous civil lawsuits have been filed and remain pending in both state and federal court. The suits seek both injunctive relief and damages. Individual plaintiffs have filed suits as have organizations like the Concerned Pastors for Social Action and the ACLU. Most notably there are several class action suits filed by teams of attorneys with significant resources. These include a suit seeking to prevent Flint residents from having to pay for undrinkable water, and another that seeks to hold the city and state financially responsible and require restitution to those affected. Claims against the state run from the decision to switch Flint's water source to the failure to act timely once resulting problems became clear.

At the outset, MCRC recognized these efforts and sought to avoid taking any action that would either hinder or duplicate the efforts of the agencies, groups and individuals who were performing them. We have been cautious not to make it more difficult for those processes to find the truth and hold those responsible accountable. For this reason, we did not subpoena reluctant witnesses, nor did we question witnesses about specific acts or decisions that related directly to the presence of lead in Flint's drinking water.

This Commission instead identified areas of concern that were not being fully addressed by others and for which the Commission and Department were uniquely able to act in the interests of Flint residents. It identified two.

First, the Commission observed that considerable resources were being devoted to meeting people's immediate needs for things like bottled water, test kits and instructions. Information was being distributed door to door and a website had been created to distribute important information and instructions. The National Guard was assisting in state efforts, and volunteers were responding by the hundreds if not thousands. However, the MCRC questioned whether these efforts were reaching everyone. The MCRC therefore resolved to direct its efforts (along with those of the Department) to ensuring that all those affected were provided equal access to information and supplies.

Our efforts in this respect are ongoing, but have resulted in tangible changes including providing information in multiple languages and clarifying that proof of citizenship was not required to receive bottled water for those exposed to the lead contamination. There were also less tangible changes in the way uniformed personnel were deployed so as to not frighten people who need assistance in a way that prevents them from getting it.

---

[6] *See e.g.,* Paul Egan, *Costs of Schuette Flint investigation hit $2.3 million,* Detroit Free Press, <http://www.freep.com/story/news/local/michigan/flint-water-crisis/2016/10/13/costs-schuette-flint-investigation-hit-23-million/92004330/> (accessed February 10, 2017).

Second, the Commission observed that while considerable resources and enormous effort were also being expended to determine how the contamination was allowed to happen and who was at fault, there was one series of questions being asked, by Flint residents and others, that was not being addressed in these investigations. Was the Flint water crisis a racial issue? Did racism, or the vestiges of racism, contribute to the crisis? Had people's civil rights been violated?

The Commission resolved to hold three public hearings and asked the Department of Civil Rights staff to examine these questions. This report is the result of that inquiry.

It is not our intent to review the scientific findings of what caused the Flint water contamination nor the other physical ills that followed. We do not seek to lay blame at the feet of any individual actor, and do not allege any specific act of overt racism. Rather, this report focuses on the interlocking role of race, economic inequality, structure, wealth, opportunity, institutions, power, and segregation of space that led to Flint's decline and served as a prelude to this crisis. The underlying and essential roles of race, racialization and racism cannot and will not be ignored in this report.

We also do not in this report allege a specific violation of the Elliott-Larsen Civil Rights Act, or other civil rights laws which this Commission enforces. To the contrary, we believe this report establishes that current state civil rights laws appear inadequate to address the deeply embedded institutional, systemic and historical racism that we find at the root of this crisis.

We do not rule out the possibility that there could be a valid civil rights claim. Whether an individual has a claim cannot be answered through a report like this, or based upon testimony at a public hearing. Even if there were a basis to allege a specific violation, substantiating the violation would require identifying a responsible party and providing them with due process before any such conclusion could be reached.

Proving a race-based violation of civil rights statutes in most instances requires an act of overt racism or one motivated by racial animus. Even in areas like housing discrimination where policy that is neutral on its face may constitute a violation if it disparately harms minorities, it is not *illegal* discrimination under state law unless the policy has no legitimate basis, or the same goal could be accomplished by other means without having a disparate impact. To date, including the testimony we have received through this process, we can make no such findings.[7] Still, the Department will continue to receive and review claims, and each will be evaluated and determined based on its own particular facts and circumstances. (Note: Any such claims could also be brought to a federal agency or filed directly in court.)

---

[7] There are also substantial issues relating to timeliness when racism is partly historical, and of possible 11th Amendment immunity when state government is involved.

One cannot fully understand the water crisis, without first understanding how Flint became a largely abandoned and distressed urban center where an emergency manager was deemed necessary. And one cannot understand Flint's current distress without understanding the central role of race. There were and still are racialized policies, practices, cultural norms and institutional arrangements that help create and maintain racially disparate outcomes. We focus throughout the report on how these forces served to perpetuate what john a. powell refers to as "structural racialization."[8]

When it comes to understanding the "Flint Water Crisis," we use terms like *racism* and *structural racism* with some caution because we recognize they are often closely linked to personal animus, or intent. In contrast, structural racialization refers to how people organize around structures that produce discriminatory results, without themselves possessing any personal animus. We believe structural racialization better reflects how interinstitutional arrangements and interactions serve to marginalize people to produce racialized outcomes.

At the same time, we do not seek to use any particular definition exclusively. We recognize that there will be some overlap of terms like structural and systemic or racialization and racism

throughout this report. Our goal is to use the term that best fits the particular context discussed and best reveals how the framework of structural or systemic racism is deeply interconnected and entrenched in our society. Similarly, discussions around housing, employment, tax base and regionalization are interconnected.

They share some causes and effects, and each continues to play a part in creating municipal distress. Taken as a whole, racialization connects the past and present, and aids in understanding how we systemically keep producing and reproducing racially disparate outcomes.

All of which brings us back to the underlying purpose of this report. Even if the civil suits result in victim compensation and the replacement of pipes, the criminal investigation brings all those responsible to justice, and the emergency manager law is eliminated or amended to include public input, it would not begin to solve the fundamental problems that led to this water crisis. Nor will it prevent the "next Flint" crisis from striking, and disparately harming communities that are disproportionately African American.

The Flint Water Crisis provides a lens through which we can recognize the complex merger of racialized structure, overt racism, racial history and disparate impact. We will explore the

---

[8] See, e.g. fn 17.

framework of structural racism embedded in Flint and Genesee County by focusing on housing, environmental justice and the emergency manager law, and by explicitly addressing the legacy of systemic and spatial racism. This crisis offers a painful lesson, one that will be repeated if we do not learn from it.

II. TERMS AND CONCEPTS

A. Implicit Bias

<u>WHAT WE DON'T KNOW CAN HURT US.</u>

Throughout our hearings, and featured prominently in nearly any analysis of the Flint Water Crisis, one question is asked more than any other. Would things have been different if this had happened in a place like East Grand Rapids, Birmingham or Ann Arbor?

Certainly, nothing that has been uncovered to date suggests that anyone intended to poison the people of Flint. Nor is there presently any evidence that anybody considered elevated lead levels to be acceptable because Flint is a city primarily made up of people of color. We want to believe, and indeed it is likely true, that nobody ever specifically even considered the race, income, or national origin of the people in Flint as factors in their decision making. All of their decisions were, as we commonly say, "colorblind."

Yet it is difficult to find anybody outside government who does not believe that at least some decisions would have been made differently if the community affected looked more like Birmingham and less like Flint.

> *"If this was in a white area, in a rich area, there would have been something done. I mean let's get real here. We know the truth."*[9]

And neither the poor decision making nor the colorblindness was limited to government decisions leading to the use of the Flint River as a water source. Immediately after the switch, people complained about the water quality. The complaints could not have been dismissed as imaginary – the water physically looked, tasted and smelled foul. Nor were the complaints isolated or attributable to a few trouble makers – they were widespread and raised by community groups as well as individual citizens. Even after some tests showed there was a problem, decision makers questioned the tests, not the water.

Again, to date there is no evidence or reason to believe that employees in the Governor's Office or the Departments of Environmental Quality (DEQ) or Health and Human Services (DHHS), consciously disregarded or discounted the complaints of Flint residents because of their skin color or socio-economic standing. We have neither seen nor heard anything that would lead us to believe that anyone in government permitted something they believed to be harmful to continue because of the racial makeup of Flint.

---

[9] Yolanda Figueroa, Flint resident, Hearing 1 @ 2:39:07.

Yet we all intuitively believe that, if government did something resulting in brown, smelly, foul tasting water being pumped into an affluent white community, the story would have a different ending.

Asked why they addressed environmental justice in their report, Ken Sikkema, co-chair of the Governor's Flint Water Advisory Task Force, explained:

> There was this question that everybody was asking, and that was; "Hey, if this had happened in an upscale, white, community, like (frankly) where I live, would this have happened?" I mean everybody on the street was asking that question, and by asking the same question, everybody had the same answer. The answer was "no, it probably wouldn't have." So we felt we had to address it in some way, shape or form.[10]

It wasn't just the initial decision makers. We know people in Flint raised objections to many of the decisions that resulted in them being poisoned. They even took to the streets in protest. Large numbers of people complaining about visibly tainted water being pumped into their homes would seem to be newsworthy. At one point the State of Michigan office building in Flint even provided water coolers and bottled water to state employees (including those of the Michigan Department of Civil Rights). And yet nothing was done.

While there was some media coverage, it was occasional and cursory. The limited coverage begs the same question of the media that we ask of decision makers: Would things have been covered differently if it wasn't Flint? Might the story have led the news, would stories have been more extensive? Most critical, would reporters have pushed government officials to provide acceptable answers? Those who made decisions on what stories to cover and how to do so will doubtlessly insist that race played no part in their decision making, that such factors were not considered at all.

While not as frequent or extensive as it could have been, there was sufficient media coverage to ensure that most, if not all, of us were exposed to at least a couple of news stories showing people protesting about the brown, smelly, foul water in Flint.[11] And yet nothing was done.

Many of us still have vague memories of having watched, read or heard these stories. Others may not even remember them at all. But most had some awareness of what was happening at

---

[10] Hearing 3, session 2 at 54:44.

[11] *See, e.g.,* William E. Ketchum III, People take to streets to protest Flint water quality, MLive news, February 14, 2015. Available at <http://www.mlive.com/news/flint/index.ssf/2015/02/flint_residents_protest_citys.html > (accessed February 10, 2017).

some point. Our lack of memory speaks to the level of importance we ascribed to 'those' people in Flint at the time, not that they didn't exist.

All of this begs a question: if we believe that race was not even considered by decision makers, how can we also believe that it played a role in the decisions they made? Research into how the human brain works suggests that race played a role in the Flint Water Crisis precisely *because* it was never considered. That it is so deeply entrenched in the very fiber of society that we have normalized what occurs in communities that are "primarily of color" and poor.

Kimberly Papillon (a nationally recognized expert on medical, legal and judicial decision-making) has delivered over 300 lectures nationally and internationally on the implications of neuroscience, psychology and implicit association in human decision-making. One of those presentations was to this Commission and the Michigan Department of Civil Rights in 2015.[12]

Papillon and others explain that most Americans agree that racial and ethnic discrimination is wrong but yet this consensus has not translated into decision-making that reflects those values. This apparent conundrum can be explained by research showing that "the operation of

---

[12] Ms. Papillon has also done presentations in Michigan for judicial associations and the State Bar of Michigan focusing on decision-making in the law. She serves as regular faculty at the National Judicial College and has been invited to speak to state and federal judicial groups at all levels, including the U.S. National Council of Chief Judges of the State Courts of Appeal, D.C. Court of Appeals, National Council of Juvenile and Family Court Judges, and the judiciaries of more than 20 states.

In addition to decision making within the legal system Ms. Papillon also focuses on decision making within governmental bodies. Her expertise in the later is evidenced by invited presentations to the United States Securities and Exchange Commission (SEC), United States Department of Justice, and United States Department of Education. Ms. Papillon also lectures to city, county and state law enforcement nationwide, addressing both leaders in police departments as well as police officers.

prejudice and stereotyping in social judgment and behavior does not require personal animus, hostility or even awareness. In fact, prejudice is often unconscious, or 'implicit.'"[13]

"Implicit bias" refers to stereotypes or attitudes that operate without an individual's conscious awareness. Research shows that individuals experience implicit bias toward a broad range of historically disadvantaged groups, often referred to as "out-groups," or those who are disadvantaged "with respect to race, ethnicity, nationality, gender, social status, and other distinctions."[14] In addition, a number of instruments have used the implicit bias test developed

by the Harvard's *Project Implicit*[15] test page, where one can find tests for gender, race, and other biases.

According to these measures, implicit bias is widespread and has a significant negative impact on African Americans.[16] The research demonstrates that implicit biases against non-whites are held throughout the country and affecting virtually every profession, even judges. For example, a study of federal district judges found that, consistent with the population, 87.1% of white judges showed strong implicit attitudes favoring whites over blacks.[17] *(Appendix B contains additional implicit bias testing information and resources.)*

Together these tests establish a number of things about our brains, including:

- Every one of us has implicit biases and stereotypes. They vary in subject and degree from person to person, but we all have them.
- These biases and stereotypes unconsciously affect the way our brain physically processes information, and they unconsciously influence our decision making.

---

[13] Curtis D. Hardin & Mahzarin R. Banaji, *The Nature of Implicit Prejudice: Implications for Personal and Public Policy. Behavioral Foundations of Public Policy,* at 13 (Princeton U. Press 2013).

[14] *See* John T. Jost *et al., The Existence of Implicit Bias is Beyond Reasonable Doubt: A Refutation of Ideological and Methodological Objections and Executive Summary of Ten Studies That No Manager Should Ignore*, 29 Res. Org. Behav. 39 (2009).

[15] Project Implicit, <https://implicit.harvard.edu/implicit/education.html> (accessed February 10, 2017). Additional details on the science behind these and other tests can be found in the research section of the Project Implicit website at <https://www.projectimplicit.net/index.html> (accessed February 10, 2017).

[16] *See* Kristin A. Lane et al., *Implicit Social Cognition and Law*, 3 Ann. Rev. L. & Soc. Sci. 427, 437 (2007).

[17] *See* Jeffery J. Rachlinski et al., *Does Unconscious Racial Bias Affect Trial Judges?*, 84 Notre Dame L. Rev. 1195, 1210 (2009).

- Because these biases and stereotypes are unconscious, they influence our decisions unless we consciously prevent them from doing so.
- Because we all have some degree of unconscious biases and stereotypes based upon skin color, being consciously "colorblind" is also consciously accepting that our thoughts and decisions will be influenced by our unconscious biases and stereo types.

Thus the initial question (would this have happened in Birmingham?) is the wrong one. Our current economic conditions, political system, and a history that includes racism all combine to ensure that events like the Flint Water Crisis will not occur in places like Birmingham. Antidiscrimination laws fail to account for the built-in biases and associations that exist beneath the conscious surface. Asking whether the result would be the same if this happened in an upper-middle class white neighborhood doesn't tell us what went wrong, and more important, it does not tell us how to prevent it from happening in places like Flint again, and again.

Even the U.S. Supreme Court has acknowledged the existence of implicit, or unconscious, bias. Writing for the majority in *Texas Dept. of Housing and Community Affairs, et al. v The Inclusive Communities Project, Inc.*, Justice Kennedy states:

> Recognition of disparate-impact liability under the FHA [Federal Housing Administration] also plays a role in uncovering discriminatory intent: It permits plaintiffs to counteract unconscious prejudices and disguised animus that escape easy classification as disparate treatment. In this way disparate-impact liability may prevent segregated housing patterns that might otherwise result from covert and illicit stereotyping.[18]

B. Racialization, Structure, Systemic Racism

Even more significant than implicit bias is the role that structures and interinstitutional arrangements play in producing racialized outcomes like the Flint Water Crisis. John Rawls, in *A Theory of Justice* (1971), wrote that if we want to know if a society is just or fair, we must look at its institutional arrangements. We must move toward an analysis that goes beyond the individual and toward a system that is dynamic and perpetuates itself.

john a. powell in his article *Understanding Structural Racialization* states:

> We need to take the focus off intent, and even off conscious attitudes and beliefs, and instead turn our focus to interventions that acknowledge that

---

[18] *Texas Dept. of Housing and Community Affairs v. Inclusive Communities Project, Inc.*, 576 U.S. ___, 135 S.Ct. 2507, 2522 (2015)

systems and structures are either supporting positive outcomes or hindering them.[19]

Today, we see racially disparate outcomes in the areas of health, education, income, transportation, housing and the environment. Structures not only distribute opportunity but also help create self-identity and community identity. It is in understanding the role of structure that one is able to understand why racial disparities persist in almost every area of institutional forms that exist in our community. Historically, these forces served to perpetuate notions of white supremacy most evident in institutions of slavery, Jim Crow segregation, and now in the racial spatial divisions that occur geographically in Michigan and across the country.

A. Racialization and Structural Racialization

Even more significant than implicit bias is the role that structures and interinstitutional arrangements play in producing racialized outcomes like the Flint Water Crisis. If implicit bias describes how our brains are wired in ways that unconsciously skew our decision-making at the individual level, terms like racialization, structural racialization, and systemic racism describe how our institutions and institutional policies do essentially the same thing.

The University of Ohio's Kirwin Institute, begins an explanation of its "systems based approach" to questions of racial inequity, with the caption "Racial inequity can persist even without racist intent"[20] Structural racialization helps explain how this is not only possible, it is pervasive.

> "The idea that racial inequity can be eliminated simply by rooting out acts of individuals is a remnant of the pre-civil rights era."

The idea that racial inequity can be eliminated simply by rooting out acts of individuals is a remnant of the pre-civil rights era. As described by john a. powell, one of the foremost authorities on structural racialization, unless directly addressed and corrected, prior racist policies will continue "echoing around" in the present, even after the racist intent of the past

---

[19] powell, john a., *Understanding Structural Racialization*, Clearinghouse REVIEW Journal of Poverty Law and Policy (Sep/Oct 2013) at 147.

[20] Kirwin Institute, *Structural Racialization; A Systems Approach to Understanding the Causes and Consequences of Racial Inequity*, (2012) available at http://kirwaninstitute.osu.edu/docs/structural-racialization_5-24-12.pdf (accessed February 15, 2017).

no longer exists.[21] Instead of viewing conditions as isolated or due to a particular policy, we must look deeper and view these conditions as systemic, group-based and interconnected.

Another important effect of structural racialization is that unlike overt racism, it is imprecise. Understanding how race and racism become racialized helps explain how "[o]nce in place, these structural arrangements have a profound effect not just on people of color but on whites as well."[22] We need to look at how individual acts link to the larger setting in which we live and work. This requires an examination and reexamination of relationships, reactions, and feedback that produce and reproduce racialized outcomes. We recognize that our structures and systems distribute benefits, burdens and racialized outcomes unevenly.

As will be shown later in this report, this last point is never more evident in housing and spatial racism. The cliché "there goes the neighborhood" was not always a punchline, but neither was it only spoken by racists. It reflected an economic reality created by structural racialization. Long after the vestiges of past racism had been racialized, and irrespective of the presence of individual racists, property values would persist in dropping based upon the presence of even a single African American family. White property owners, regardless of their own personal beliefs and practices, were thus also the victims of racism. In fact, as powell has noted in other contexts, the "impact may have even been greater, in absolute numbers, on whites."[23] While even overt racism can have white victims, racialization's focus on a "systems based approach" to questions of racial inequity helps us understand how whites can be participants in perpetuating systems and structures that actually harm themselves.

As Nils Gilman wrote in *What Katrina Teaches about the Meaning of Racism*:

> Long after white people cease to actively hate and consciously discriminate against racial minorities, there persist social patterns – where people live, which social organizations they belong to, what schools they attend, and so on – that were built during the hundreds of years where active racial prejudice was the fact of ethnic life in America. These social and institutional structures, in other words, are constructed on prejudicial racialist foundations. As such, they are bearers of the racist past, even though they may today no longer be populated by active bigots. This social

---

[21] powell, *Understanding Structural Racialization* at 150.

[22] *Id.* at 146.

[23] powell, john a., *Deepening Our Understanding of Structural Marginalization*, Poverty and Race, Vol. 22, No. 5, September/October 2013, at 4.

and economic exclusion on the basis of race is what "racism" is really about.[24]

As we use the terms in this report, 'racialization' describes how past racism has embedded itself into our social and political structures so as to perpetuate and reproduce racially disparate results. 'Structural racialization' further describes how multiple structures work together to produce results that are not only cumulatively more harmful, but also have no clearly identifiable cause and therefore no simple solution.

Because our legal system is built around the notion of identifying and then holding bad actor(s) responsible for bad outcomes, it often does not provide the tools necessary to address bad outcomes that lack either a clearly identifiable cause or intentional animus. As powell explains: "In many ways, our laws have not yet caught up with this framing either. Time and time again we have seen the courts struggle to find a racist behind the curtain, struggling with the concept of disparate impact."[25]

Today, we see racially disparate outcomes in the areas of health, education, income, transportation, housing and the environment. These disparities cannot be explained using only language that describes racism, and racists. Today's disparities often cannot be attributed to individual acts or specific causes, they are often the result of the complicated relationship between numerous factors, policies and causes that interconnect to produce and reproduce unintended, but no less real, racial disparities and unjust harms that extend even beyond race. Understanding the role played by structures and institutions is thus critical not only to understanding today's disparities, but also essential if we ever wish to address their causes. Structuralized racialization suggests that fixing these problems will not only require that our laws and policies be changed, but also the way we look at the problem to begin with.

As stated by john a. powell:

> We need to take the focus off intent, and even off conscious attitudes and beliefs, and instead turn our focus to interventions that acknowledge that systems and structures are either supporting positive outcomes or hindering them.[26]

B. Other terms

---

[24] Nils Gilman, *What Katrina Teaches about the Meaning of Racism*, SSRC (June 11, 2006), <http://understandingkatrina.ssrc.org/Gilman/> (accessed February 10, 2017).

[25] *Understanding Structural Racialization, supra* at 148.

[26] *Id.* at 147.

1. Crisis

The people of Flint were poisoned with lead.

That sentence alone establishes that this is a crisis. But labeling it a crisis has political and social overtones. It is also a disaster, but unfortunately for the people of Flint, it does not fit the definition of disaster that enables the city to receive federal disaster relief. It is a catastrophe, a horror, and a tragedy of unfathomable dimensions. Perhaps most accurately what happened in Flint was a fiasco, "a complete failure" of government.[27]

The Civil Rights Commission will continue to use the word *crisis* to define the events in Flint. While the definition may not be exactly correct, the term has the benefit of having become a commonly used and recognized way of referencing the harm that befell the people of Flint. More important, when disasters and declared states of disaster occur, they are cleaned up and declared over. Declaring an end to a disaster may be appropriate for events that result from outside forces, though many of the people affected may still be dealing with the "disaster" for some time thereafter. Government, however, caused this crisis and therefore government should not see this as a disaster that can be followed by a short period of recovery and then ended. Government's responsibility here is not merely to help people address *their* problems – because the problems were caused by government. Government's responsibility is deeper. This *crisis* will continue for many years to come.

2. Flint Water Crisis

We also choose to formally identify the crisis as the Flint Water Crisis. Repeatedly, the term "water crisis" is preceded by "Flint." Everyone recognizes the reference. Flint may yet have another water crisis as, even when this contamination is gone, the pipes replaced, and the water safe, its price will likely be beyond the financial reach of many of Flint's residents, but the impact of this crisis will, both physically and non-physically, be long lasting.

3. Genocide, overt racism, criminal conduct

Some would like us to call the crisis genocide – we cannot. Genocide is a deliberate and organized effort targeting the extermination of a (racial/political/cultural) group. To date, we are not aware of any evidence to suggest any sort of deliberate targeting or intent to harm. Others want us to call the government officials involved in causing the crisis overtly racist. Again, we have found no evidence as of the release of this report to support that claim.[28] Nor has the MCRC found any evidence that suggesting that what happened was intentional or deliberate. Furthermore, if it can be shown that conduct was deliberate, we expect that it will

---

[27] Merriam-Webster Dictionary, as found at <https://www.merriam-webster.com/dictionary/fiasco>.
[28] We do not find that there was no overt racism, only that to date we have not found evidence to establish it played a roll.

result in additional criminal charges being filed by the Attorney General, whose office is conducting the criminal investigation.

4. Racism and racists

The Commission finds that racism played a significant role in creating the conditions that allowed the lead contamination to happen, and in the failure to recognize and address it in a timely fashion. Racism is referred to as the combination of race, prejudice, and power.

We avoid the use of the word "racist" in this report. This should not be interpreted as a finding that it doesn't apply. Rather, we believe that there is a lack consensus on a common definition of the term. If racist is only used to describe a person who overtly discriminates based upon a belief in white supremacy, then we have not found evidence it applies here. However, if racist is defined to include anyone who does anything that could be considered racism, then the word could rightfully appear throughout this report. As we have said and will repeat, racism does not require malicious intent.

Calling a person a racist, changes the debate from a constructive review of the facts to gain a better understanding into a defensive argument that impedes any potential for progress. The role that race played in creating this crisis is too significant, and the need to recognize the role that racism plays in how public policy is developed and implemented is far too important, to permit the issue to become an irreconcilable semantic argument about what makes someone a racist.

The Commission will, however, use the word racism when we believe it to be appropriate. We do so because we will examine specific concepts like "environmental racism" and because it is the only word that properly describes some conduct.

5. Systemic racism vs. structural racism and racialization

Systemic and structural racism are very similar concepts, and are often used interchangeably. When they are differentiated, the term structural is generally used in a way that relates to racialization.

We will use the term systemic rather than structural because we want to draw a clear distinction between that which is racialization, and that which has become systemic. We view structural racism as a facially neutral (or colorblind) policy that produces racially influenced outcomes across institutions and society. When it is possible to point to where in the system's ostensibly colorblind structure the race-based results are being produced, that structure has been racialized. When the policy produces racially disparate outcomes, but the cause is not formally built into the policy or decision-making structure, the problem is systemic.

For example, if a subdivision and adjacent country club both had official policies that excluded African-Americans, the policies would be racist.

If at some point the subdivision felt pressure to change its racist policy, changed it to limit residency to families that would also join the club, the subdivision's policy would have been racialized. The subdivision's policy no longer contains anything overtly racist, but it is structured to achieve that goal. It doesn't matter if the subdivision actually was formed by non-racist golfers who only wanted to live with other golfers, or even if requiring club membership was intended to keep out low income residents. The subdivision's policy may be colorblind, but by limiting residency to members of a whites-only club, its structure has been racialized to produce the same racist results as before.

If at a later point the club also drops its whites-only policy and replaces it with one that admits anyone based on the recommendation of a member and vote of membership, both the subdivision and club will have policies that appear colorblind, but could continue to produce the same racially predetermined outcomes.

The club's membership policy would no longer overtly discriminate, but by restricting membership to only those "approved of," any actual integration would require active participation by the majority of the same members who adopted the prior policy.

Similarly, without a conscious effort, the subdivision is likely to remain all white. Persons of color are unlikely to feel welcome in a neighborhood simply because the law permits them to be there, especially one whose existing residents had previously banned them. African Americans would also feel unwelcome if the police stop and question people of color because they 'look out of place,' especially if this continues after the first black families have moved into the subdivision.

Thus, even after the structure has been purged of any mention of race and it is technically possible for blacks to join, former policies and practices will often systemically continue to produce the same results. There is no longer a policy that discriminates and racial exclusion may not be anyone's intent, but left unchecked "the system" produces discriminatory results anyway. Accepting the results without taking appropriate steps to correct the system (perhaps advertising in minority newspaper and radio advertising) is systemic racism.

Another example would be a large retail business that has only white employees, though located in a diverse community. It may never have intended to discriminate nor had a discriminatory hiring policy, but if the business has always hired the family and friends of its existing white employees, it will probably have only white employees. Again, "the system" is producing discriminatory results. Recognizing the results without challenging, and taking reasonable steps to counter them, is systemic racism.

II.   Housing: The Roles of Racialization and Spatial Racism in Creating Institutional Racism

A. Introduction: "What's past is prologue."[30]

It is not sufficient to view the pumping of contaminated water into the homes of Flint families as an engineering failure. We need to understand what precipitated the conditions under which such a failure was possible. Preventing the "next Flint" requires understanding its roots. As more contemporaneously stated by Steve Jobs, "You cannot understand what is happening today without understanding what came before."[31]

> "...the Flint Water Crisis did not begin with the decision to temporarily use the Flint River as a water source or joining the Karegnondi Water Authority..."

Events leading to the Flint Water Crisis did not begin with the decision to temporarily use the Flint River as a water source or joining the Karegnondi Water Authority to use Lake Huron water as a permanent source. Nor can it be viewed as starting with the appointment of an emergency manager.

When telling the story of Flint, the common narrative is of a city that rose to the highest of heights on the back of the automobile during the first two-thirds of the 20th century, and then crashed along with the auto industry in the century's last 30 years.   This is a simplified, sanitized, version of history written from a white person's perspective.

The story may be accurate, in so far as it goes, but it does nothing to explain why the story of the City of Flint is so different than the story of the County of Genesee. It does nothing to describe how the residual wealth created by those working in the automobile industry is spread out everywhere except within the city limits – yet at the same time the residual costs of that era are still being borne primarily by those who live there.

---

[29] Faulkner, William. *Requiem for a Nun*, Act 1, Scene 3 (1951).

[30] Originally from William Shakespeare's *The Tempest* (Act 2, scene 1), this quotation is engraved on the National Archives Building in Washington, D.C., the National Archives and Records Administration is the government agency tasked with preserving America's historical documents and records.

[31] Co-founder of Apple, as recorded by historian Leslie Berlin.

Crediting, and then blaming, the automobile industry for everything may explain the rise and fall of Flint as an economic powerhouse, or its prominence on the national and international stages. But, if the automobile industry was the sole cause of Flint's downward spiral, the same would be seen throughout Genesee County. The collapse of the automobile industry, as well as the relocation of its production, have had a dramatic effect on all those who directly or indirectly depended upon it for employment. But at its peak, the auto industry also created much wealth and great municipal resources. Where that wealth and those resources went is very much a part of Flint's story.

In the fifty years between 1920 and 1970, Flint's population grew 111% from 91,535 residents to 193,317.[32] In the forty years that followed the numbers fell just as quickly, and by 2010, the number of people calling Flint home was roughly what it had been in 1920. Thus looking at just total population numbers, census data does seem to support the idea that Flint and the automobile share a common storyline unique to the industrial age.

Upon a deeper examination of Flint's census data, one begins to see a more complicated story. One that involves not only industrialization and deindustrialization, but also government policy, individual self-interest, and skin color. All of which had profound impacts not only on the city of Flint itself, but by determining the opportunities that were or were not available, also on the lives of Flint's residents.

In 1920, Flint was almost exclusively white. Today, after the total population doubled and then fell back under 100,000, more than half Flint's residents are African Americans. During the 1970s, the city's black population grew from roughly 54,000 to 66,000, while its white population sank from 138,000 to 90,000. Even as the oil crisis crashed the automobile industry and drove the Flint's total population down 17%, its number of black residents went up 22%. Thus, the city's history cannot be explained simply by blaming decreasing auto manufacturing.

An even greater problem with pinning Flint's demise wholly on the fate of the automobile is illustrated by contrasting the city's census population data with that of the county.

Like Flint, Genesee County's population rode the roller coaster up during the boom years. Its population during the years of 1920-1970 grew more than 250% from 125,580 to 444,341. Although Genesee County's population saw some decrease since its highpoint in 1980, but it never dipped below 425,000 residents. Between 1970 and 2010, while Flint saw nearly half its residents leave the city, Genesee County as a whole saw a decrease of less than 5%.[33]

---

[32] All population figures are from U.S. census decennial reports.

[33] Some of whom were living in southern Genesee County and may have been working in Oakland County.

Flint's history is laid out in great detail by Andrew R. Highsmith[34] in his dissertation *"Demolition Means Progress: Flint, Michigan, and the Fate of the American Metropolis,"*[35] and later in his book by the same name.[36] We rely heavily (both as specifically cited and generally) on Highsmith's work gathering and documenting the facts that have allowed us to look back in time.[37]

The history of Flint's rise and fall cannot be fully told without including the very significant roles played by both government-sanctioned public policy and opportunity-driven private decisions; and how each was intertwined with race, racialization, and racism.

B. 1900-1930: The need to "remind Black people of their position"

Almost from the moment of the founding of General Motors in 1908, the City of Flint "suffered" from growing pains. U.S. Census figures show the city's population at the beginning of the

---

[34] Andrew R. Highsmith is a specialist in modern U.S. history with particular interests in metropolitan development, public policy, racial and economic inequalities, and public health. He is an Assistant Professor of History at the University of California, Irvine.

[35] Andrew R. Highsmith, Demolition Means Progress: Race, Class, and the Deconstruction of the American Dream, a dissertation submitted in partial fulfillment of the requirements for the degree of Doctor of Philosophy (History) in the University of Michigan (2009), available at < https://deepblue.lib.umich.edu/bitstream/handle/2027.42/62230/ahighsmi_1.pdf> (accessed February 10, 2017).

[36] Andrew R. Highsmith, Demolition Means Progress: Flint, Michigan, and the Fate of the American Metropolis (Historical Studies of Urban American) (Chicago: University of Chicago Press, 2015).

[37] Our citations will be to the Hightower dissertation unless specified otherwise.

century at 13,103. The 1930 census shows the city had grown to 156,492 residents, a more than tenfold increase in just thirty years.[38]

In 1930, more than 80% of Flint's residents were native-born whites.[39]   Nearly two-thirds of this group was originally from Michigan, with the others divided about evenly between people from nearby Midwestern states and those from southern states. Approximately 14.2% of the population was foreign born, the majority of whom came from English speaking countries. Less than 4% of residents were African-Americans.[40] Residents of Asian and Hispanic descent together made up only about 1%.

The absence of people of color can in no small part be attributed to General Motors as both an employer and developer. Prior to the outbreak of World War II, the only GM jobs available to blacks were either janitorial or in the foundry,[41] the latter widely considered to be among the worst jobs possible. GM was also very involved in building new homes to support their growing workforce and, as with homes sold by other developers, all sales included racially restrictive covenants.[42] It is, however, not clear to what extent GM wished to impose such restrictions on Flint, and to what extent they merely reflected the wishes of the city's residents.

GM produced its first million cars between 1908 and 1919.[43] In 1919 GM organized the "Modern Housing Corporation" to attract and house the employees needed to feed their continuing growth. Between 1919 and 1933, GM's Modern Housing division built nearly 3,000 new homes in three newly created Flint neighborhoods (Chevrolet Park, Civic Park, and Mott Park). The homes in these neighborhoods were built to attract desired employees, and were not made available to the public market.[44]

The homes were modern, well-constructed and reached by new streets and sidewalks. They came with landscaping, sewer, water, gas, and electric service. Those who could buy the homes

---

[38] Nearly three quarters of Genesee County's 211,641 residents lived in the City of Flint.
[39] Highsmith dissertation at 43.
[40] *Id.*
[41] *Id.* at 64.
[42] *Id.* at 44.
[43] *Id.* at 40.
[44] *Id.* at 59.

could do so on very favorable terms, including 10% down payments, 6% interest and monthly mortgage payments of 1% of the amount borrowed.[45]

All sales also came with legally enforceable restrictions ensuring that the neighborhoods would never permit commercial establishments (except doctor and dentist home practices), multi-family dwellings, livestock, liquor sales, or outhouses. Also prohibited was permitting any property to "be leased to or occupied by any person or persons not wholly of the white or Caucasian race."[46] While government actions or policies were not involved, the underlying doctrine of separate but equal found in the 1896 U.S. Supreme Court *Plessy v Ferguson*[47] holding also served to shape Flint.

Arthur E. Raab Realty Company was the exclusive seller for GM lots and homes. During the early 1920's they advertised that "Each Home owner will have a Homesite at least 50 by 100 feet, with all improvements and with ample restrictions to protect his Home and to secure the maximum of beauty, utility and value. No shacks, huts or foreign communities will be allowed."[48]

> "...racial covenants and prohibitions were the rule, not the exception..."

Such racial covenants and prohibitions were the rule, not the exception, irrespective of the developer or realtor. Throughout this period and into the 1940s, virtually all new construction included restricted deed covenants.[49] Even when not expressly spelled out, realtors would reassure nervous purchasers by noting that all real estate transactions were subject to the rules of the National Association of Real Estate Boards (NAREB). They would then point out that NAREB had a code of "ethics" that prohibited the selling of property in segregated white neighborhoods to non-whites.[50] This racial separation was in no way limited to real estate, it was in keeping with everyday life in Flint. Life in Flint was to be lived according to a "Jim Crow" type system.

---

[45] *Id.* at 58.
[46] *Id.* at 59, citing Scott Peters, *History of Mott Park Community*.
[47] *Plessy v. Ferguson*, 163 US 537 (1896).
[48] *Id.* at 59-60.
[49] *Id.* at 57.
[50] *Id.* at 63.

GM's establishment of employment barriers for black workers was anything but unusual. While GM limited the possibility of employment to only a few of its least desirable jobs, downtown Flint retailers refused to hire African American workers at all. White-owned barbershops, restaurants, bars and hotels also refused to serve black customers. These practices were well entrenched - Flint's highly renowned Durant Hotel didn't permit a black guest until 1954.[51]

Throughout this period of Flint's history, movie theaters, amusement parks, skating rinks, bowling alleys, and other places of public accommodation were open to black patrons only during designated times or in restricted spaces, if it all. At the Michigan Theater, black moviegoers were restricted to the balcony. Bands at the IMA Auditorium presented two shows, 9-midnight for whites, with blacks not welcome until 1 am.[52]

Flint's elected officials also regularly donned blackface and participated in minstrel shows to raise money for charity. While ostensibly for charitable causes, the message sent when elected officials "blacked-up" for such performances was not subtle. "Jim Crow performances were used to remind black people of their position."[53]

Perhaps the clearest message of how Flint viewed black people's "position" was the one sent by the Bernston Field House public swimming pool. Six days per week the pool was for the use of whites only, while black children were relegated to sprinklers the city would set up across the street. Blacks were allowed to use the pool only on Wednesdays. Every Wednesday night the pool was completely drained and everything was cleaned, so the facility would again be ready for those who were allowed entry on Thursday morning.[54] The "necessity" to empty and clean a swimming pool based on the skin color of the previous users was an outright symbol of racism.

> "...being white bestowed certain benefits not available to African Americans."

This Commission believes it is critical to remember these early years of Flint's history when being white bestowed certain benefits not available to African Americans. They are an important part of a long legacy of racism and segregation upon which everything that follows is built.

Flint's African Americans did not make up 4% of the total population until sometime after 1930. Yet well before then, this small portion of the population was already subject to the spatial

---

[51] *Id.* at 64-68.
[52] *Id.*
[53] Black Flint resident Mary Helen Loving, Hightower dissertation at 68.
[54] *Id.* at 66-7.

exclusions that would soon create strictly defined segregated black sections of the city. As time passed, a white family could argue that preventing a black family from moving into the house next door was about protecting the value of a financial investment. However, the same cannot be said about the refusal to permit that family from purchasing something from their store.

Beginning in the 1930s, the federal government also implemented decisions that racialized its housing policies. It is the same racialized economic "reality" that was the dominant factor in creating the white flight of the 1960s.

C. 1930s: Depression, racism, racialization, and redlining

Two significant events took place during the 1930s that profoundly impacted Flint, the latter of which continues to reverberate today: the Great Depression and the creation of Home Owners Loan Corporation (HOLC).

1. Racism

Although GM founded its Modern Housing Corporation in 1919 largely to address a housing shortage fueled by its growth, housing construction could not keep up with the rising population. This lead to severe overcrowding of existing housing stock within the city, forcing residents to move into tents, boxcars, tarpaper shacks and similar "homes of the homeless."[55] Overcrowding also gave birth to sprawl, with self-built homes being constructed in areas ringing the city where land was cheap and building regulations non-existent.

One study of housing during this period found that inside the city most land parcels were at least 35 feet wide and required houses be worth at least $600. Outside the city, there were no minimum lot sizes and no zoning restrictions or building codes, resulting in "smaller and smaller lots which are sold without [building] restriction for $1 down and 50 cents a week."[56] What both had in common was that land sales came with strict racial restrictions.[57]

When the Great Depression hit at the end of 1929, it hit Flint hard. Before its official end in 1939, automobile manufacturers cut production by up to 75%, unemployment rates in Flint

---

[55] *Id.* at 46.

[56] *Id.* at 231, quoting journalist John Ihlder. John Ihlder, *"Flint: When Men Build Automobiles Who Builds Their City?" Survey 36* (September 2, 1916), 549.

[57] *Id.* at 231.

hovered at nearly 50%, and more than half of Flint's families received public aid relief.[58] Public aid for African Americans living in the Floral Park and St. John neighborhoods exceeded 85%.[59]

While the Great Depression and resulting unemployment provided temporary relief from overcrowding, it greatly exacerbated the problems presented by already deteriorating living conditions. Some families left, largely families from the south who decided to return to the states from which they had come. Many more stayed, often relocating to self-made homes in the rural areas surrounding the city where they could throw up a tarpaper shack and grow food to help sustain themselves through the tough times. By the end of the decade, the city lost about 5,000 residents, while the county population grew by more than 20,000.[60]

In 1934, area researchers, city planners, real estate developers and GM officials, together with the federal Civil Works Administration (CWA), conducted a detailed survey of Flint housing. CWA surveyors visited and assessed each of the city's roughly 35,000 dwelling units.

In addition to documenting high occupancy rates caused by the shortage of housing, they found the existing housing often in poor repair, and unsanitary living conditions.[61] They found nearly 15% of the city's housing units required major structural repairs, and at least 2% were described as uninhabitable and warranted immediate demolition. About 20% of the homes had no working baths, 13% lacked toilets, 25% lacked hot water, and at least 6% had no running water at all.[62] However, these problems did not exist in every part of the city. In fact, 98% of the housing in the city's west side (white) neighborhoods was in good repair.[63]

The CWA survey broke the city down into six distinct neighborhoods representing the different conditions presented by different parts of Flint.[64] The contrasts between these six neighborhoods present an illuminating snapshot of life in Flint in the 1930s.

---

[58] *Id.* at 47-48.
[59] *Id.* at 54, fn 24; citing Erdmann D. Beynon, *Characteristics of the Relief Case Load in Genesee County, Michigan* (Flint: Genesee County Welfare Relief Commission, 1940), 47.
[60] *Id.* at 235.
[61] *Id.* at 49.
[62] *Id.* at 48.
[63] *Id.* at 51.
[64] *Id.* at 50.

- In Flint's far north, there was an area described as a "low grade peripheral white section, started as a series of cheap subdivisions and inadequately provided with such urban facilities as sewers, sidewalks and paving." The area shared much with the "shanty towns and blighted areas" that ringed the city limits.[65] Its development lacked both planning and building standards, and as a result the often self-built housing was of "flimsy construction." The area lacked good utilities and city services. Its residents were largely uneducated and exclusively white.[66]

- On the city's west and near northwestern sides, were two areas that included upper middle-class, and other high to medium grade white neighborhoods, including Civic Park, Mott Park, and Glendale Hills. These premier neighborhoods on Flint's west side contained much of the city's most modern homes, solidly built, and in good repair. The homes had access to all municipal services and utilities. Residents were well-educated skilled autoworkers, tradespersons, retail workers, and professionals with "few machine operators or unskilled workers" and virtually no immigrants from outside of northern Europe. They were also "almost entirely white"[67]

- To the southeast there were a number of transitional neighborhoods near the city's downtown commercial core made up of older homes. Although it included neighborhoods like Grand Traverse, which had previously been "aristocratic," this area had seen large homes converted to rental units and the introduction of rooming houses and commercial structures. Even though the population included many well-educated skilled workers and professionals, its proximity to more neglected and rundown areas of the city and the possibility this signaled the encroachment of Negroes, southern European immigrants, and other "undesirable" social groups, the future of these transitional neighborhoods was questionable.[68]

- On the eastern edge of downtown Flint was the Woodlawn Park neighborhood, the city's most exclusive residential enclave. Made up of well-built homes and mansions, 98% of which had been built in the previous ten years, this area was home to GM's top shareholders and executives. In the Flint of the 1930s, it was "considered today's

---

[65] *Id.* at 51, quoting Weidner, *"The Housing Problem in Flint,"* 2.
[66] *Id.* at 51.
[67] *Id.* at 51-2.
[68] *Id.* at 52.

aristocratic section." Although this neighborhood also bordered the "older, undesirable section" with its dilapidated housing, Woodland Park's social exclusivity, high prices, and the most carefully drafted restricted racial exclusions, assured that its future was not at risk.[69]

- On Flint's near north side was the St. John neighborhood described as "a deteriorated residence section, more than a third negro, adjoining and partly enclosing a part of the Buick factories." It was where unskilled factory workers lived, along with small business owners, professionals, and those working as domestics in the adjacent Woodland Park. Although older than the modern construction, the quality of housing in St. John was superior to that in several more highly-rated sections of the city. Still it was deemed inferior to those areas based largely the observation that "Nativity is highly mixed." St. John was home to "negroes largely from the south and a large number of white occupants from central, eastern and southern Europe. There [were] also a considerable number from Asia Minor and from Mexico." In addition to its poor housing stock, the St. John neighborhood was highly polluted by the adjacent factories. It was also specially isolated, wedged between Buick factories, the rail line and the Flint River, it was a very defined and finite space that already contained the largest concentrations of both poverty and African Americans.[70]

- Floral Park was just south of downtown Flint where free persons of color and former slaves had settled when they first arrived in the mid-19th century. Blacks in Floral Park were limited to living in just one small part of the neighborhood, near the rail lines. Poverty and dilapidated housing were worse than other neighborhoods, with the exception of St. John. Although black residences were rigidly segregated, Floral Park as a whole was economically diverse and included domestics, shopkeepers, and a growing number of unskilled and semi-skilled GM factory workers. No matter how bad poverty or housing got in Floral Park, the better air quality and proximity to downtown meant life for African Americans living in Floral Park was always better than it was in St. Johns. Floral Park was the more desirable, and for African Americans it was where you lived *if you could.* This created a social divide between blacks living in the two communities.

The CWA survey found that poor housing, like poverty, was present everywhere in Flint, but nowhere were they more severe than in St. John and Floral Park.[71] Because these two areas also were home to almost all of Flint's 6,000 black residents, the study documented the correlation between poverty, poor housing, declining value and deteriorating living conditions

---

[69] *Id.*
[70] *Id.* at 53-6.
[71] *Id.* at 54.

and race. However, the study failed to note that African Americans moved into these two neighborhoods because racially exclusive land restrictions   prohibited them from living anywhere else. Although the study noted the overcrowding present in these two neighborhoods, it failed to recognize that the overcrowding resulted from compelling an ever-increasing population to live in a rigidly defined and finite space.

The segregation of Flint's African American population was not the result of "race neutral," or even race conscious but arguably non-discriminatory practices. Instead, Flint's segregation prevailed due to a number of factors, including:

- It was during a time when Jim Crow tactics were prevalent, legally sanctioned, and very public; white people did not want to interact with, no less live near, black people.

- "Separate but equal" was an accepted legal theory as enunciated by the U.S. Supreme Court in *Plessy v Ferguson*.

- Legally enforceable and plainly racist restrictions were included in all land sales and excluded blacks from living other than were they were permitted to.

- Realtors could lose their licenses for the "ethical violation" of showing a house in a white neighborhood to a person of color.

It is this "spatial segregation" that caused Professor Hammer to recall the maxim that the difference between northern and southern racism is that while "in the south you can be close, but not equal -- in the north you can be equal, but not close."[72]

2. Racialization and redlining

The second seminal event in the early 1930s is less well known then the Great Depression, but plays an even more significant role in understanding the origins of the Flint Water Crisis and why a disproportionate number those effected were both African American and financially stressed.

The Home Owners' Refinancing Act (HORA), also known as the Home Owners' Loan Act, changed the way American's viewed home ownership and shaped the concept of home financing as investment. It initiated a federal housing policy that would grow and provide opportunity to (most) Americans. It also changed the way Americans viewed and discussed race.

President Franklin D. Roosevelt signed HORA in 1933 in response to the Great Depression. The Act was part of the "New Deal" being offered to Americans. It was hoped that jump starting the nation's real estate market would help accelerate the economy overall, while also

---

[72] Hammer testimony at Hearing 2, 23:20.

addressing the growing problems faced by Americans who were unable to find housing, forced to live in inadequate and unsanitary housing, and even losing the homes they had purchased.

HORA's goal was to stem foreclosures and boost construction. To do so, it created the HOLC, which purchased delinquent home loans from lending institutions, and then refinanced the homes with new loans that were long-term, low-interest, and fully amortized. Reducing foreclosures in this way saved banks and other lending institutions from financial losses while also protecting families from losing their homes.[73]

Between 1933 and 1936, HOLC purchased delinquent loans and then refinanced mortgages for more than 20% of America's owner-occupied residential properties.[74] Millions of Americans literally bought into the idea that mortgages no longer needed to be the short-term, high-interest loans, with higher monthly payments followed by a large balloon payment at the end.

Though long-term loans with low down payments were great for home purchasers, there was a reason they hadn't already become the norm. It was a great risk to lend money without knowing that the property could be foreclosed and sold for more than was owed in the event that payments were not being made. Full amortization of the loan assured the lender of a profit if payments never became an issue, but there was no protection if the property value went down. The key to ensuring long term loans could be profitable was ensuring loans were only made on properties that would hold or increase their value. Put plainly, properties needed to be in financially secure neighborhoods.

To identify properties that were 'safe' to loan money against, the HOLC inquired how local real estate experts made similar assessments. Thus, the new federal agency requested that Flint forward the 1934 CWA survey to them "at the earliest possible moment."

Apparently, the federal administrators at HOLC liked what they saw, and quickly designed a formal nationwide rating system to assess neighborhoods to determine which ones provided the financial security necessary to support a mortgage on its homes, and which ones did not.

For areas like Flint, HOLC would literally create "residential security maps" outlining and then rating each neighborhood in the metropolitan area (the city itself as well as the surrounding suburbs). Flint's residential security map eventually had 50 such residential areas.[75]

In Flint, as in many places, HOLC contracted with local realtors to create residential security maps by individually rating each neighborhood on an A, B, C, D scale. The most "secure"

---

[73] Hightower Dissertation, *supra* at 71.
[74] *Id.* (farmlands not included)
[75] *Id.* at 75.

neighborhoods would be rated A, and outlined and shaded in green on the map, while B and C neighborhoods would be delineated in blue and yellow respectively. The least desirable neighborhoods, and thus the least secure for long-term loans, were rated D and outlined and shaded in red.[76]

Because these maps were created for the specific purpose of identifying which neighborhoods would support a long-term mortgage, it was easiest to get a mortgage on a house in an A neighborhood. Homes located in D neighborhoods, those outlined and shaded in red, were not eligible for the government's amortized, long-term, low-interest loans. These neighborhoods would come to be identified as *redlined*, and is the origin of the term *redlining.*'[77]

To ensure consistency, HOLC instructed property surveyors, HOLC officials and local realtors throughout the U.S. that assessed and scored neighborhoods to classify each neighborhood using eight criteria:

1. Demand, including both sale and rentals.
2. Percentage of home ownership.
3. Age and types of structures.
4. Economic stability.
5. Social status of residents.
6. Availability and adequacy of utilities.
7. Proximity to schools, businesses and houses of worship.
8. Deed, and zoning restrictions sufficient to protect the neighborhood from inharmonious social groups and incompatible land uses.[78]

The fact that none of these criteria is explicitly racial did not make the intent any less clear. Similarly, in HOLC's instructions to those determining ratings, criteria for receiving an A or B did not explicitly reference race. The pretense was however largely dropped when it came to HOLC's instructions for C and D ratings.

In addition to criteria like the poor physical condition of houses and lack of utilities, HOLC's description of C neighborhoods included those without racially restrictive housing covenants, thus undergoing an "infiltration of a lower grade population." C ratings were for "neighborhoods lacking homogeneity."

D-rated neighborhoods were described as severe housing decay and widespread influx of nonwhites. These "redlined" neighborhoods where HOLC loans would be impossible to get were "characterized by detrimental influences in a pronounced degree, undesirable population

---

[76] *Id.* at 72.
[77] *Id.* at 72.
[78] *Id.* at 73.

or an infiltration of it, low percentage of home ownership, very poor maintenance, and often vandalism present."

Federal lending policy had officially and formally adopted policies that "redlined" areas for having "undesirable" or "lower grade" populations, or those who lacked deed restrictions to keep such people out. Federal loans would be denied to people whose neighbors lacked "homogeneity."

Lest there be any confusion about HOLC's policies, it provided those visiting and rating neighborhoods with instruction sheets. Raters were to consider things like zoning, utilities, parks and recreation, transportation, and nuisances. Nuisances were defined to include "such things as obnoxious odors, noises, traffic conditions, (and) fire hazards…" as well as "encroachments of apartments, commercial or industrial properties." Also warranting a lower rating, under the definition of "nuisance" were "infiltrations of lower grade population or different racial groups."[79]

Overcrowding and depression ensured that the City of Flint did not fare well overall in 1937. Only two neighborhoods received an A rating. An additional seven neighborhoods received a rating of B, and 18 more were scored as C. These 27 neighborhoods shared one thing in common - not one of them had any African American residents. African Americans were restricted to just three of greater Flint's 50 districts, all of which were rated D.[80]

Moreover, all but one of the neighborhoods that bordered the three with black residents was rated either C or D. The one that did receive a B was a part of Woodland Park where middle- to upper-class business executives lived in mostly newly built homes. Although raters specifically noted that this neighborhood was "too close to 'C' and 'D' areas to the west," it had sufficient protections in deed restrictions, a clearly drawn color line, and "pride of ownership" that it was ultimately decided that in spite of the proximity, this neighborhood "will hold up."[81]

Clearly the presence of African Americans was not the only way to be redlined. Twenty all white neighborhoods also received D ratings. However, these D-rated neighborhoods, which included most of the still underdeveloped suburban land surrounding the city, earned their D's due to a lack of building and zoning regulations, and poor municipal and utility services. The distinction is critical. The poor scores in these areas told developers and municipal governments what they needed to do to improve their scores so that new residents would be able to secure financing. This incentive drove much of the development that came in the 1940s and beyond, even making white flight possible by providing places to flee to.

---

[79] *Id.* at 74-5.
[80] *Id.* at 75-7.
[81] *Id.* at 76-7.

Building on the success of the long term, low interest, and fully amortized loans offered by HOLC, Congress passed the National Fair Housing Act (NFHA) in 1934 and thereby created the Federal Housing Administration (FHA). While HOLC was created to allow the federal government to purchase loans (initially out of foreclosure), FHA would instead insure loans offered by banks and other lending institutions. By insuring rather than purchasing the loans, a much larger market could be reached and more homes would be built. While HORA and HOLC addressed a problem created by the depression, NFHA and FHA would create and drive new development, thereby not only reviving, but also growing the real estate, housing, banking and construction economies. [82]

Naturally FHA needed to address the same impediment to lending that HOLC did. To make offering long term, low interest, amortized loans profitable, loans needed to be secured by property that would hold or increase in value. Following HOLC's example, FHA developed detailed and predictable guidelines to determine whether both the house and the neighborhood were of sufficient quality to be a safe enough investment for the federal government to insure it and limit the lenders' risk.

Due to the breadth of the FHA mortgage insurance program and its strict guidelines, FHA's system for determining how housing quality and purchasers' credit worthiness effected a mortgage's risk quickly became the national standard. The use of these same FHA guidelines to determine what areas of a city like Flint were safe enough to qualify for FHA-insured mortgages not only controlled the neighborhoods in which banks would finance purchases, but also where developers would build the homes.[83]

The FHA also created underwriting manuals describing in greater detail the formulas to be used to rate a neighborhood pursuant to the published guidelines. They not only required factoring in things like sufficiency of utilities, adequate transportation, the age and condition of buildings, and neighborhood appeal, but also "protection from adverse influences" and neighborhood "stability." Each criterion would be given points by appraisers and the points would then be amalgamated to determine a neighborhoods score.[84]

Like HOLC, FHA used this score to rank the neighborhoods on a scale of A to D, with D-scored neighborhoods rejected from loan consideration. And, like HOLC, FHA treated investment security and racial integration as mutually exclusive. And finally like HOLC, if the FHA system

---

[82] *Id.* at 83.
[83] *Id.* at 82-7.
[84] *Id.* at 85-8.

itself was not sufficiently explicit, the guidelines, instructions and guidance provided to its assessors removed any doubt about the intent.

One official in FHA's Economics and Statistics Division instructed assessors that neighborhoods that were to be "rejected" as being "undesirable for loan purposes" should include "all blocks in which there are more than 10% Negroes or race other than white; [and] areas in which there are a considerable number of Italians or Jews in the lower income group."[85] At the other end of the spectrum this official indicated that "where rents are high, the percentage of owner occupancy is high, the condition of the buildings good and there is no race other than white, there will be found areas that rate high for loan purposes."[86]

Grade D, or "reject," neighborhoods where FHA insured mortgages could not be offered, were those that had "an intermixture of races and nationalities." Grade A neighborhoods were those with "no residents of a race other than white nor of a nationality on a lower economic scale than the old American stock."[87]

The FHA also made clear that even a very good neighborhood should be downgraded if a lower grade neighborhood was growing in its direction. Further, proper zoning and deed restrictions must be in place if a neighborhood was to avoid "infiltration."[88] It was perhaps most straightforward in its 1938 FHA Underwriting Manual, which instructed that "If a neighborhood is to retain stability, it is necessary that properties shall continue to be occupied by the same racial group."[89]

HOLC and FHA programs were enormously successful, both nationally and in Flint. In 1933, the City of Flint issued just 13 permits for new homes. In 1940 (following the 1934 creation of the FHA), that number was 629. By the end of the 1940s, annual new housing permits grew to almost 1,000.[90] In 1937, nearly 99% of Flint homeowners held long term, low interest, amortized loans that were not available in 1933.[91]

---

[85] *Id.* at 85, quoting EPA official Homer Hoyt, "*Instructions for Dividing the City.*"
[86] *Id.*
[87] *Id.*
[88] *Id.* at 86.
[89] *Id.* at 87.
[90] *Id.* at 138.
[91] *Id.* at 71.

But obtaining the loans to finance this growth meant that African Americans arriving in Flint, and those already there, needed to be kept in the neighborhoods where they already lived. Based upon the 1940 census data, Flint was the third most segregated city in the country and the most segregated city in northern states, and even more segregated than all but two cities in the south.[92]

The foregoing marked a turning point on the road to the creation of what the 1968 Kerner Commission[93] described as "two Americas." Racism had already created strictly enforced racial segregation in places like Flint, but the 1930s turned this racism into federal policy. The path forward was now set; the American dream of property ownership was going to be made available to only *some* Americans.

Racism that had previously been practiced by individuals was now incorporated in government policy through carefully crafted language. While still rooted in the identification of some as "undesirables," it was officially no longer about the animosity; it was now about protecting investments. Racial separation no longer required racist actors because the *system* had been racialized to do it automatically.

Lending rules and standards created in the 1930s soon became the fuel powering suburban sprawl. New housing was developed in spaces that were racially restricted to whites only, financing required staying one step ahead of any spatial integration. In order to attract residents, suburbs would have to protect peoples' investment in homes by creating quality infrastructure and schools, and by keeping people of color out. To protect your investment, if you *could* move, you *should* move – but only *some* were allowed to do so.

It was official government policy: If you were white, the government would ensure that you could only purchase homes that would increase in value; homes with modern infrastructure and access to good schools. The government would then help you make the purchase.

---

[92] *Id.* at 63, (Only Miami, Florida, and Norfolk, Virginia, were worse.)

[93] National Advisory Commission on Civil Disorders, "Report of the Commission on Civil Disorders" (1968). The National Advisory Commission on Civil Disorders, known as the Kerner Commission after its chair, Governor Otto Kerner, Jr. of Illinois, was appointed by President Lyndon Johnson in July 1967 (as the rebellions in Detroit and Flint were winding down) to examine the causes of the "racial disorders" then plaguing America and identify possible actions to prevent them from recurring. A pdf of the report is available at <https://www.ncjrs.gov/pdffiles1/Digitization/8073NCJRS.pdf> (accessed February 15, 2017). An official summary of the report is available at < http://www.eisenhowerfoundation.org/docs/kerner.pdf> (accessed February 15, 2017).

However, if you were black, government policy instead ensured that your very ownership of a home made it, and those located near you, less valuable. In theory, you had an equal right to obtain a mortgage, but you could only secure one on a home where you were not permitted to live.

The rules that would shape America as it moved out of the Great Depression, and through World War II, were set. They were racialized, systemic, and supported by government policy.

D. 1939-1945: WWII, racialized segregation, and spatial racism

World War II brought a quick economic turnaround, as depression-era Flint quickly became an "arsenal of democracy." In announcing the U.S. intent to support but not join the British in battle, President Roosevelt, indicating the need to produce "more ships, more guns, more planes -- more of everything," called upon "American industrial genius... to put every ounce of effort into producing these munitions."

As automobile manufacturers retooled plants to produce the tools of war, ever increasing numbers of new employees were required to perform new functions. GM alone created 25,000 new jobs in greater Flint before the war ended. Flint no longer had an unemployment problem; it now suffered from a shortage of employees.

The labor shortage was not unique to Flint. The nationwide shortage of manufacturing workers only grew as 1941 progressed, and was significant enough to create new job opportunities for black workers. Some black advocates viewed this as an opening to demand a federal ban on employment discrimination. Fearing that such activism could get in the way of his push to maximize war related manufacturing, and perhaps recognizing that racial discrimination in employment could be slowing the effort, President Roosevelt issued Executive Order 8802 in 1941.[94]

---

[94] A. Philip Randolph, president of the Brotherhood of Sleeping Car Porters, had met with President Roosevelt the previous September. At that time Roosevelt said he would consider the requests for both equal employment laws and desegregation of the armed forces. With no agreement and no action, Randolph gained support from tens of thousands of African Americans for a march on Washington. When the two met again two weeks before the march was to take place, this order was the precondition Randolph required before canceling the march. Executive Order 8802 of 1941 is available at <http://sdpb.sd.gov/EducationalServicesGuide/etvprograms/pdf/HistoryofBlackA/FDR's%20Executive%20Order%208802.pdf> (accessed February 10, 2017).

Executive Order 8802 of 1941 decreed that "as a prerequisite to the successful conduct of our national defense production effort . . . there shall be no discrimination in the employment of workers in defense industries or government because of race, creed, color, or national origin." The Order created the Fair Employment Practices Committee (FEPC) within the existing Office of Production Management. Although the Order lacked real enforcement powers, it was nonetheless effective in getting the message out. Government officials negotiating contracts with automobile executives persuaded the manufacturers to begin hiring people of color at defense facilities.[95] At Buick alone, hundreds of black workers, who previously held some of the worst manufacturing jobs, were able to transfer to less arduous, higher paying positions on the assembly line."[96]

As the war effort continued, and especially after the U.S. entered the war after Pearl Harbor and otherwise employable workers were deployed, previously impenetrable bars for African Americans seeking better employment opportunities continued to be broken down.

By the end of the 1940's Flint's African American population had doubled - from just under 7,000 in 1940, to 12,000 in 1947, to just over 14,000 in 1950. By 1960, that figure reached nearly 35,000.

The geographic space into which this growing

population moved, however, remained static. With both racialized government financing policies and the private and legally enforceable racial exclusions, deed restrictions, and covenants firmly in place, it didn't matter that many African American factory workers were now earning more. Black people still had no choice but to move to Floral Park or St. John.

Still, within that static space, little was structurally changed. During the seven years ending in 1947, when population grew by 5,000, only 25 new homes were built for African Americans. Predictably, all were within the St. John and Floral Park districts.[97] Renters fared no better than those looking to purchase. With more people looking for fewer units, rents started to rise.

---

[95] Highsmith at 179-80.

[96] *Id.*

[97] *Id.* at 140. By the end of the decade more than 4,000 city building permits would be granted for houses in racially restricted subdivisions.

> "The racialized rules adopted in the 1930s proved to be as effective
> as the racism of the 1920s."

The racialized rules adopted in the 1930s proved to be as effective as the racism of the 1920s. The cumulative and compounded effects served to systemically disadvantage African Americans. Spatial racism had become entrenched.

1945-1967: Postwar Boom, Opportunity, Sprawl, Competition, Compression, and Rebellion

1. Postwar Boom brings opportunity and opportunity begets sprawl

If you, your parents, or their parents, grew up and attended school in suburban America during the 1950s and 60s, it is almost certain they were there because of federal housing programs, that you are where you are now at least in part because these programs existed, and you are white.

Most American families made their biggest strides forward in financial security, social status, and education during the 1940s and 50s. The existing government mortgage programs were joined postwar by similar provisions in the G.I. bill.[98] When these programs were used to purchase a new home, families began to consider the purchase not just a home, but an investment. As contemplated by the government mortgage programs, the home gained value, creating wealth and a source of equity for all future purchases. During this same period, education became more accessible, both through the G.I. bill and through the quality of the public schools that came with a government supported move to the suburbs.

These programs were the key that opened the future for many who succeeded. Certainly, there were exceptions. Some whites climbed the economic ladder without benefit of these programs, as did some African Americans, but they were exceptions to the rule.

This was, as Tom Brokaw would later label them, the "Greatest Generation," made up of people who won World War II and "who have given us the lives we have today" and "the America we have today."[99] They had saved the world for democracy, made America a "superpower" and returned from victory with intent of continuing to shape America's destiny and claiming their piece of it. Individually and collectively, we owe much of what we are to their legacy.

---

[98] The Servicemen's Readjustment Act of 1944 is commonly referred to as the G.I. Bill. The Act was signed by President Franklin D. Roosevelt on June 22, 1944, and provided returning WWII veterans with funds for medical care, unemployment insurance, higher education, and housing.

[99] Brokaw, Tom, "*The Greatest Generation*" Random House (2004). From the introduction.

When Japan attacked Pearl Harbor on December 7, 1941, African Americans were already less well off than Americans as a whole, mostly as the result of private acts of racial discrimination and slavery's legacy. During the war they fought no less heroically than any group of Americans, at least to the extent they were allowed to. Yet after World War II they were systematically denied the opportunities for economic advancement that the federal government provided to white Americans. The roads to a better future were not open to *all* Americans.

During this time, Flint issued record numbers of building permits. By the end of the 1940s, 838 new homes were built in the Woodlawn Park and Brookside neighborhoods, and 750 in the Woodcroft neighborhood. In addition to these more established city neighborhoods that had scored well on HOLC and similar residential 'security' maps, some 4,000 new homes were also built in previously redlined areas on the outer edges of the city, as those neighborhoods added city water, sewer and other municipal services. As mortgages became increasingly contingent on not just the security provided by segregation, but also the availability of municipal services, building began to follow the pipes.[100]

At first, whites looking for more space and more modern housing did not have to go far. By 1947, financing a home without indoor plumbing was next to impossible, but extensive water and sewer service was not yet extended or constructed outside the city. As a result, while the suburban areas were planning and building infrastructure, the new construction was largely within the city limits. An FHA report noted that: "In the post-War years, home building became more firmly tied to water and sewer lines and to Government minimum property requirements for mortgage insurance. This revived a concentration of building in the City of Flint."[101] The 1953 report further stated that Flint "is just now beginning to spill over its legal boundaries in a conventional urban sprawl."[102]

But is wasn't only whites moving into Flint. The war had opened decent paying jobs to African Americans and they came in record number. By 1955, 18,000 African Americans lived in Flint, triple the number who were there when WWII broke out just 15 years earlier. (It would grow

---

[100] Highsmith at 138-139.
[101] *Id.* at 137, quoting Federal Housing Administration, "*An Analysis of the Flint, Michigan SMA (Genesee County) as of January 1953.*"
[102] *Id.*

close to 35,000 in the 1960s.)[103] Color lines having held with few exceptions, they inhabited roughly the same St. Johns and Floral Park neighborhood.

City inspections in 1954 and 1955 not only discovered dilapidated and unmaintained structures, there was also extreme overcrowding, including: 4 adults and 7 children sharing a basement accessible via a single trap door in one instance, and 5 room apartments shared by 24 and 19 people in two others.[104] Condemning structures when it was necessary, only made matters worse.

Landlords who hadn't left the market were not shy about taking advantage of the situation. Median rents went from $25 in 1940, to $47 in 1955, and $75 by 1955.[105]

Black and white populations were both growing. Whites just had more space into which to grow. 'Urban sprawl' captures only half the story.

> 2. First baby steps away from segregation bring negligible change and introduce 'block busting'

Civil rights advocates made some progress during this period. Advocates had opposed the FHA's blatantly segregationist policy from its inception, and in 1947, the FHA finally relented and eliminated all explicit references to race contained in its official *Underwriting Manual.*[106] However, while this may have made "open occupancy" FHA's *written* policy,[107] it had little effect on the ground in Flint.

Private restrictions at the local level continued to ensure white neighborhoods stayed white as new homes were constructed and purchased. However, for blacks, although the FHA policy change made mortgages theoretically possible, "race neutral" considerations intended to protect the value of a loan's collateral, made loans almost impossible to get a mortgage in the overcrowded, deteriorating neighborhoods that discrimination had created. "Transitioning" neighborhoods were of course never "secure investments."[108]

---

[103] *Id.* at 326.
[104] *Id.* at 327.
[105] *Id.* at 325.
[106] *Id.* at 143.
[107] *Id.*
[108] *Id.* at 142-144.

The U.S. Supreme Court provided a bigger victory in 1948 when it decided two cases in which state supreme courts had allowed judicial enforcement of private race-based covenants restricting the sale of land.[109] While the cases were consolidated under the name of a Missouri case, it is notable that the other case was from Michigan.[110] In the Michigan case, lower courts instructed purchasers who were "not of the Caucasian race" to vacate a house in Detroit based upon a restrictive agreement between the prior owners and neighbors.[111] The Michigan Supreme Court upheld the finding ordering the Sipes family to move out of their purchased home and neither use nor occupy it in the future. Not only were racial restrictions between private parties permissible, they could be judicially enforced if even a third party later violated the agreement.[112]

The U.S. Supreme Court ruled that the racial restriction could *not* be judicially enforced. However, the court made it clear that while it was unconstitutional for state courts to enforce the restrictive agreements, "the restrictive agreements standing alone cannot be regarded as a violation of any rights guaranteed to petitioners by the Fourteenth Amendment."[113]

This landmark Supreme Court ruling had little initial effect in Flint. Since the FHA continued to include racial integration as a mortgage risk factor into the 1950s, and because private homeowners, builders, realtors and lenders all continued to keep housing segregated by race, judicial enforcement of segregation was largely unnecessary to its preservation. African Americans remained unable to purchase homes outside the limited neighborhoods others had defined as appropriate for them.

During the first half of the 1950s, less than 100 of the almost 6,000 newly constructed homes in Flint were built for African Americans, and not one of them was built outside the neighborhoods consigned to blacks.[114]

Moreover, even if race was no longer specifically mentioned in FHA policy, FHA underwriters continued the practice of assuming that the presence of blacks and integration negatively impacted nearby property values into at least the late 1950s, and homeowners, builders, realtors and lenders continued such practices into the 1970s. Even today, after the self-

---

[109] *Shelley v. Kraemer*, 334 US 1 (1948).

[110] *Sipes v. McGhee*, 316 Mich. 614, 25 N.W.2d 638 (Mich. 1947)

[111] *Sipes* at 620-621. Based upon trial testimony that "he appears to have colored features . . . and she appears to be the mulatto type."

[112] *Id.* at 631.

[113] *Shelley* at 13.

[114] Highsmith at 144.

fulfilling prophesy that the existence of a black neighbor by itself devalues property has been disproven countless times in numerous locations, the myth and fear continues. It has been indelibly burned into our collective consciousness and is now unconsciously practiced.

3. Sprawl preserves spatial separation and begets political competition

In the United States we like to compete. Capitalism is itself built on the theory that incentive provides the best motivation for developing the 'new and improved,' because it pays to be first. Rewarding 'winning' makes all competitors better, the reasoning goes, because merely coasting along guarantees being passed by the competition. Progress is assured by the desire to win, and the fear of losing. Incentive drives development, development serves everybody, winning and losing is determined by merit.

a. The Tiebout model

In post WWII America, the notion that competition between entities caused them all to be at their best was incorporated as public policy. The model, first put forward by economist Charles Tiebout, theorizes that smaller competing government entities will allow potential residents select from a municipal smorgasbord of differing services and then select a community where they would only pay taxes for what they wanted and tax money would be used efficiently.[115]

In essence, the Tiebout model treats local government like a business. Whether one thinks the model succeeded in creating good local governments is an opinion that may depend on whether you are someone local governments desire, or you are not. It is a Darwinist business approach to government that ignores the inability of the losing government to declare bankruptcy and to go work for the winner. Ultimately, the Tiebout model ran into the same problems that other efforts to run government like a business have. The business model is constructed on creating winners and losers. In good government there aren't supposed to be losers, or at least government's goal should not be to create them.

b. Residential sprawl

The period that followed WWII was a time of opportunity and wealth for America as a whole. During the 1950s urban sprawl accelerated and the American Dream was symbolized by a home in the suburbs surrounded by a white picket fence. As discussed previously, flight was first fueled by a growing white population as new arrivals moved into homes, rentals, and neighborhoods being vacated by those moving up. It was also largely restricted to areas served by city water and sewer. That would soon change and the Tiebout model helps explain why.

---

[115] Richard C. Sadler and Andrew R. Highsmith, *"Rethinking Tiebout: The Contribution of Political Fragmentation and Racial/Economic Segregation to the Flint Water Crisis,"* Environmental Justice 9(5), (2016) at 2.

By the end of the 1940s, it was all but impossible to secure financing for a home without water and sewer, which meant that whites moving away from the city's urban core were not able to go very far. As the FHA mentioned in its 1953 report, the city "is just now beginning to spill over its legal boundaries in a conventional urban sprawl."[116] But soon, urban sprawl accelerated, due to the push of blockbusting and 'white flight', and the pull of the security and services provided in suburban enclaves.

Prior to this time, houses, shacks, and garage homes outside the city limits were not purchased with financing. The absence of building codes was a source of serious concern. The *Flint Journal* in 1955 reported that "families are permitted to move into homes that have curtains strung up instead of partitions, no doors on bathrooms and bedrooms, no finished flooring, the electrical wiring in but little else."[117]

Throughout the 1950s, the number of people wishing to flee the byproducts of urban living increasingly looked outside the city limits, seeking cheaper land than was available in the popular subdivisions inside the city. As they did, water and sanitation became bigger and bigger problems for those living in "the fringe." Building homes outside the city meant that water would have to be obtained from private, or in a few instances public, wells.[118] Sewers for the most part did not exist at all. Residents installed septic tanks, or used outhouses.[119]

Between the homes with unregulated septic systems and those with no human waste disposal system at all, suburban living could be rather unpleasant. As early as 1947, studies were observing that: "Septic tank effluent flows from the townships through Flint in nearly every direction."[120]

Meanwhile, the ever-increasing demand for water from wells was drying up the water table. As a result homeowners outside the city would often complain about poor water pressure and

---

[116] Highsmith at 137.

[117] *Id.* at 279, quoting "FAS Says Practice May Develop Slums," *Flint Journal*, September 28, 1955.

[118] *Id.* at 283.

[119] *Id.* at 281.

[120] *Id.* at 281, quoting Israel Harding Hughes, Jr., "Local Government in the Fringe Area of Flint, Michigan" (Ann Arbor: Institute for Human Adjustment, University of Michigan) (1947)

water that smelled and/or tasted bad.[121] In the mid-1950s, individual wells began running dry, and experts warned "An acute water shortage looms in the near future."[122]

That shortage would soon cause a suburban water crisis in the fast growing Village of Flushing. Even with a new public well and the imposition of water rationing, the area ran out of water early in 1954. For the remainder of the year, Flushing relied upon "Operation Taker" purchasing and transporting water by the truckload from the City of Flint.[123]

Trucking water was not a tenable permanent solution and a reliable supply of water, and the state-of-the-art system it needed was outside Flushing's budget. Flushing was forced to issue revenue bonds and charge residents higher water rates.[124]

Flushing didn't have a sewer system either. Although the ballot initiative to fund a sewer system passed on the third attempt, Village leaders worried that the one vote margin was insufficient support to proceed. Also in 1954, the Michigan Water Resources Commission threatened punitive action against suburbs without sanitary systems. Still, it wasn't until the FHA announced the suspension of new home loan approvals in Flushing that the Village Council committed to completing a full system.[125]

When the FHA then announced the lifting of its suspension and began approving loans again, the Village promoted Flushing as the right place to build, even though the costs of the two projects would fall on residents. With FHA backing, it had little difficulty convincing builders and buyers that Flushing, with "all the conveniences of the Big City," was the place to be.[126]

The lesson was not lost on other municipalities around Flint's fringe who began the expensive process of building their own water and sanitary systems. Rather than being deterred by the higher costs and taxes for these services, new residents were drawn by them. The new residents also increasingly demanded good schools and other "city" services. To protect their

---

[121] *Id.* at 283.
[122] *Id.* at 284.
[123] *Id.* at 285.
[124] *Id.*
[125] *Id.* at 286-287.
[126] *Id.*

investments, residents demanded zoning restrictions. The FHA, for its part, was not content with water and sewers, it started to tie its financing to schools, roads and sidewalks as well.[127]

Local governments who failed to provide these services paid a different kind of price. In 1957, community leaders from Clio Township met with the Director of Flint's FHA office for advice on how to spur the kind of home building and development nearby townships were enjoying. The answer was straightforward: Clio lagged because it did not offer satisfactory water, sewage disposal, storm sewers, or schools. No 'urban' infrastructure meant no home building.[128]

To ensure the character of future housing would fit the type of community they desired, local governments enacted minimum lot and building sizes. Giving residents what they wanted cost money, but the 'right' residents were willing to pay. For those residents it was money well spent, and their property values began to rise.[129]

Many community residents joined together to demand municipal services. Residents worked together for zoning restrictions based on who they wanted to join them. They joined PTAs to fight for their schools, and sometimes even worked together to fight the taxes necessary to fund such initiatives. Whatever purpose brought them together, the issues were specific to the jurisdiction. All of this led to the development of suburban identities.[130]

These identities became more fixed as marketing campaigns were launched to urge people to "shop locally," thereby keeping jobs and tax money in the community.[131] The very act of voting on local taxes sent an unmistakable message about who was part of what cluster of shared interests. People began to identify themselves by the suburb in which they lived. Ideally this new identity would rank you high on the new social structure. But whatever suburb or subdivision you lived in, one's new identity began with, "I don't live IN Flint."

Tiebout was correct. People were willing to pay for the services they wanted, and municipalities would do what was necessary to keep up with each other. That meant that those with sufficient assets to do so not only had the ability to select the services they wanted, they had the ability to restrict 'membership' to only others with similar resources. From the perspective of the local governments and their residents, it was a win-win.

---

[127] *Id.* at 251-252.
[128] *Id.* at 253-254.
[129] *Id.* at 286-289.
[130] *Id.* at 297-299.
[131] *Id.* at 299. *E.g.,* "Buy, Build, Believe in Fenton" or "Shop Flushing First."

Local development still hinged on keeping FHA approval; the Tiebout model just added the greater need to maintain a certain class of residents. Either way, African Americans need not apply.

The suburbs were growing and they would not look back. Neither would their residents.

<blockquote>c. Corporate Sprawl</blockquote>

This phenomenon was not restricted to residences. Automobile manufacturers needed to build new plants, and land was cheaper and more readily available outside the city. Residents and municipalities welcomed the tax base that plants and businesses would bring. As the Tiebout model predicted, when multiple municipalities wanted the same thing they would compete for it. Residential or commercial the power rested with taxpayers. The more one was wanted, the better the deal they could get. This would prove to be especially valuable to General Motors.

Immediately after WWII, the automobile industry prospered and Flint prospered with it. GM began a massive expansion to meet the demand created by the combination of returning service personnel and years without the production of any new cars or trucks. Initially this benefitted the City of Flint as existing plants were reconverted to civilian production. When the new Chevrolet-Fisher Body assembly plant opened in Flint Township in 1947, it almost went

unnoticed that it was just outside the city limits, meaning tax revenues would not go to the city. Flint still thought of itself largely as a region, and what was good for GM was good for Flint. By 1960, that would change as seven more manufacturing plants were built outside the city, while several plants inside the city shut down.[132]

Multiple factors led GM to build outside the city limits, not the least of which was the availability and lower cost of sufficient land to hold a large plant and related employee parking. Federal policy also played a role as it began encouraging dispersal for the "strategic safety" of key industrial, government, and other facilities "since there is no known defense against the atomic bomb itself except space." In 1950 federal tax breaks allowed for 100% deduction of costs of constructing new facilities for defense contracts. [133]

There were also forces at play that caused manufacturing facilities to move away from the region altogether. Beginning in 1953, the government's newly enacted policy of requiring all defense materials to be purchased at the lowest price incentivized moving to locations where

---

[132] *Id.* at 208-212.
[133] *Id.* at 213-214.

the unions were weakest and the wages lowest. Neither of these criteria described Flint. GM had also recognized cost efficiencies that would result from dispersing manufacturing functions nationwide. Not only was proximity to customers more convenient, it was far cheaper to manufacture where the resources were and then transport parts for regional assembly, than it was to ship finished automobiles.[134]

Lost manufacturing initially came at the expense of the older plants, thus hurting Flint first. The movement of GM manufacturing from Flint to the suburbs presents a good example of an inherent contradiction in the Tiebout model that also helped to precipitate Flint's fall. While Tiebout encourages inter-local competition, it fails to recognize that the competition it is encouraging is also intra-regional. That is, "us" and "them" are really on the same team.

When GM started to build plants outside the city, Flint supported the efforts because it thought of itself a part of a team. Never mind that it builds the plant and pay taxes in the next township, if it's good for GM it will be good for Flint. Flint was, at least in their minds, a metropolitan whole that would rise or fall together.[135]

Not only did Flint decline to protest a plant's location outside the city, it actively provided support to make it possible. Flint built roads to service the facilities and employees, and they provided water and sewer service to the plants.[136]

The suburbs with the new plants may have felt part of a larger metropolitan team at some point, but not once they started receiving the new tax revenues. Fully three-quarters of the school and local government budget in Beecher came from corporate taxes. Flint Township and other suburban jurisdictions with GM plants assessed property taxed at lower rates than their counterparts without plants – but also spent more per pupil in the schools. When asked to take a regional approach, they were not interested. This attitude exacerbated the "Flint" versus "suburbs" rift.

---

[134] *Id.* at 214-216.
[135] *Id.* at 203-204.
[136] *Id.* at 203.

d. Flint, water, and the Tiebout model

As just noted, Flint provided water and sewer services to GM plants outside the city. [137] In doing so, it financially supported its own downfall. Ironically, it provided the support because Flint believed in supporting regional partners for the mutual benefit of all.

During the 1940s and 50s, with no formal policy controlling to whom the city could supply water, the city commission approved all GM requests; GM could not proceed without the services and the jurisdiction funded by GM's tax dollars could not provide them. Until 1953, Flint also provided water and sewer services to some suburban residential customers, but discontinued the practice because of worries of insufficient capacity. However, the city continued to approve all requests from GM. [138]

Flint even provided GM discounted water rates. Industrial customers used over half the water Flint pumped, but paid only about a third of the revenue Flint received. For residential customers the numbers were reversed: they used about a third of the water, but paid half the revenue. [139] In December 1959, for example, Flint residents paid thirty-two cents per unit, while industrial users including GM facilities outside the city received a volume discount rate of just twenty cents per unit after the first 105,000 units. [140]

Flint's financial support for the suburbs and suburban plants was not without its detractors. After the city commission voted to provide water and sewer service to a new suburban Chevrolet plant, the Congress of Industrial Organizations (CIO)[141] political action committee chair summed the vote up by stating:

> In taking this action the city fathers are completing the cycle and it now appears that General Motors plants outside the city are going to enjoy all of the major services rendered by the city, including fire and police protection; water and

---

[137] *Id.* at 203.

[138] *Id.* at 218-219.

[139] *Id.* at 220, the numbers do not add to 100% because non-industrial commercial businesses were counted separately.

[140] 100 cubic feet.

[141] The CIO would later merge with the American Federation of Labor to become the AFL/CIO.

sewage disposal—everything except the doubtful privilege of paying city taxes.[142]

Still, although always a contentious process, the commission voted to supply water to GM every time it asked. They would do so because they shared GM's regional vision, and because "without GM, Flint wouldn't exist."[143]

With GM using half the water it was able to pump and an increase in population, Flint was running out of capacity by the early 1960's. In 1959, the City Commission directed the city's consulting engineers to develop a preliminary design of a project to address the water needs of the Flint area. In 1962, Flint purchased land in Worth Township to build a new pumping station as part of its plan to build a pipeline to bring in water from Lake Huron. It was then discovered that one of the city's most powerful figures (a millionaire owning real estate, coal, fuel oil, and concrete companies) had been using insider information to buy up land from unsuspecting Worth Township landowners with the intent to resell it to the city at a profit. As a result, he, the city's real estate broker, and its City Manager, were indicted.[144]

Six months later, following a set of circumstances a former County Prosecutor said had "shocked" and "stunned" him, the charges were dismissed, profits illegally earned were repaid, "the city and the public were outraged," and "Flint's plans for its own pipeline were dead." Instead, on June 6, 1964 Flint signed a contract to purchase its water from the City of Detroit.[145] Thus, Flint ended up buying water from Detroit in order to provide sufficient water for the Flint area, including GM's plants built outside the city. Yet these same plants paid taxes to help build

---

[142] Highsmith at 220, quoting R. Clark. *Flint Taxpayers Pay the Shot*, Searchlight, (April 17, 1952).

[143] *Id.* at 221, quoting City Commissioner Craig.

[144] Ron Fonger, "50 years later: Ghosts of corruption still linger along old path of failed Flint water pipeline,"mLive News service, November 12, 2012, available at < http://www.mlive.com/news/flint/index.ssf/2012/11/ghosts_of_corruption_still_lin.html> (accessed February 12, 2017); *see also* written testimony of Jeff Wright, Genesee County Drain Commissioner, CEO Karegnondi Water Authority, "The Flint Water Crisis, DWSD, and GLWA; Monopoly, Price Gouging, Corruption and the Poisoning of a City" at 2-4.

[145] Wright at 2-4.

the suburbs to the detriment of Flint. Later many of those same plants would close altogether leaving Flint and its dwindling population to pay for an oversized water infrastructure.

It appears that Flint would have had its own supply of Lake Huron water had it not been for local government corruption in 1964. Instead, the departure of industry, shift in population, decrease in tax revenue, increased water rates from Detroit's water department, etc., resulted in Flint residents paying some of the highest water bills in the country.[146] Then, in 2014, with Flint facing financial distress and the imposition of an emergency manager, government changed the source of Flint's water supply which led to the Flint Water Crisis. The Commission finds that the lack of trust in government by Flint's residents is not without good reason.

e. Race and the Tiebout model

Sprawl, with its multiple competing government units, may well have doomed Flint even without spatial or systemic racism. The idea that a region divide into separate entities with separate and often redundant infrastructures may have intended to spur competition that would make each better. However, the competition also seemed to absolve each entity of any obligation to help the other.

Sprawl, in words that would have been familiar to those participating in it, encouraged city dwellers to "Grab your coat and get your hat, leave your worries on the doorstep."[147] If there was no room within the city limits where utilities were available, build outside it and band together to provide your own services. If a manufacturing or commercial source of property tax revenues is looking to relocate, cut a deal with them to come to you. After all, some revenue is better than no revenue. Us against them.

Defenders of the Tiebout model contend that it is colorblind, even if adopting the system of dividing a region into multiple competing governments may doom urban centers like Flint. They contend that Tiebout's competition means there may be winners and losers in the region, but this will be determined on merit, not race.

Except that in Flint, it had everything to do with race. Intra-regional competition may itself be colorblind, but it was applied where established rules were, at best, racialized. To compete for families, local governments were incentivized to create exceptional educations systems,

---

[146] *Id.* at 3-6.
[147] "On The Sunny Side of the Street" (1930) music and lyrics by Jimmy McHugh and Dorothy Fields, is an American jazz standard that was made popular through the 1930s, 40s, 50s and 60s, with recordings by artists including Louis Armstrong, Peggy Lee and Benny Goodman, Fats Waller, Judy Garland, Billie Holiday, Nat King Cole, Dizzy Gillespie, The Coasters, and Doris Day.

provide drinking water and sewer access, and develop other infrastructure like libraries and paved roads. Being the best at such things would maximize residents' return on investment.

And of course, mortgage rules and residents' fears would continue to mean that one of the things a competitive local government needed to be 'best' at, was to segregate based on race, wealth, and opportunity. To developers and realtors, there were three kinds of communities; white, black and "declining."

Tiebout's model is about winners and losers – us versus them. Unfortunately, for a person of color, the rules of the game were systemically rigged so that no matter who the 'us' was, you would always be 'them.'

4. 1958: The Road Not Taken

The story of Flint is not complete without briefly addressing the failed proposal to create a "New Flint."

Unveiled in 1957, and defeated before the end of 1958, the New Flint proposal was an organized effort to consolidate Flint and twenty-five surrounding suburbs into a single governmental entity.[148]

The proposal to create a New Flint was targeted at the effects of the competitive Tiebout model which created what one critic called the "chaos of conflicting local governments, all squabbling over responsibilities instead of working together for the benefit of the whole metropolis."[149] The New Flint proposal was intended to provide the suburbs with the infrastructure resources they lacked, while providing the city with the room to grow it needed. It would have preserved the tax base and directed it at common goals, rather that providing a windfall only to the small jurisdiction where a manufacturing facility or other commercial venture was located.[150]

The New Flint proposal was supported by academic researchers, corporate leaders, city commissioners, trade unionists, and concerned citizens who viewed metropolitan fragmentation as a pressing problem. Most notably, both General Motors and the Mott Foundation (who in other contexts were often blamed for creating intra-county division) were strong supporters of the plan and advocated for its adoption.[151]

---

[148] Highsmith dissertation, *supra* at 304.

[149] *Id.* at 269, quoting Lawrence Lader, "Chaos in the Suburbs," Better Homes and Gardens 36 (October 1958).

[150] *Id.* at 267-268, 300-306.

[151] *Id.* at 306-307.

Still, opposition grew quickly. The earliest and strongest opposition came from suburbs who responded by seeking to incorporate in order to protect commercial tax revenue. The battle between Flint's desire to annex and local governments trying to incorporate ultimately resulted in the creation of Charter Townships. Local opposition to regionalization also both resulted from and encouraged the growth of individual suburban identities and anti-urban sentiment.[152] African Americans were also largely opposed to the New Flint proposal because they had not been consulted or involved in creating the plan, and because the plan would have diluted any voting power they had.[153]

Although sufficient signatures had been collected to put the proposal on the ballot, the County Board of Supervisors declined to do so. A challenge went to the Michigan Supreme Court, which upheld the Supervisors' decision in October 1958.[154] The plan was defeated without having reached the voters.

The defeat of the New Flint Plan marked an end to the movement for metropolitan or regional government in Genesee County. Rather than uniting the region, the failed effort only widened the already growing rift between Flint and its suburbs.[155]

5. Integration Breeds (Re)Segregation

Very few African Americans were able to purchase homes outside of St. John and Floral Park. The few exceptions occurred when African Americans purchased homes from willing sellers (primarily by making cash purchases or privately negotiating land contracts with individual sellers).[156] One such exception took place in the Evergreen Valley neighborhood on Flint's southeastern edge.

At the dawn of 1963, Evergreen Valley was a small all-white subdivision of just over 500 homes that were less than 10 years old.[157] In July of that year, one of the houses was purchased by an

---

[152] *Id.* at 306-311.
[153] *Id.* at 307.
[154] *Taliaferro v. Genesee County Supervisors*, 354 Mich. 49 (1958).
[155] Highsmith, *supra* at 314-316.
[156] *Id.* at 146.
[157] *Id.* at 331.

African American who moved in without incident.[158] Unwittingly, that event and the fact that the all-white residents of Evergreen Valley accepted it placed a bullseye on the subdivision and signaled the birth of *blockbusting*.

In Evergreen Valley, and soon elsewhere, blockbusting involved using each black purchase to whip up fear in nearby property owners. When homes became available, they would be shown only to African Americans, and white home-hunters would be steered elsewhere. When the home was purchased by an African American, realtors would contact nearby residents to warn them the neighborhood was in decline, the newest black neighbors were getting closer, and whites would soon be in the minority. Homeowners in Evergreen Valley increasingly received phone calls, door to door solicitors, flyers and mailings containing such 'warnings.'[159]

Evergreen Valley's white residents largely resisted the temptation to give into their fears, and many outwardly shared their desire to live in an integrated neighborhood. Neighborhood associations were formed and signs were placed on lawns saying "This House Is Not for Sale – We Like Our Neighbors."[160]

Nonetheless, such efforts eventually failed. Residents who initially fought against flight, often decided to sell when an African American purchased a home on their block. It is impossible to determine how many whites sold because they personally did not want to live next door to a family of color, and how many merely believed the self-fulfilling prophecy of declining home values had arrived on their front porch. What was certain was that whenever a white owner moved out, racial steering assured that a black owner would move in. Change it seemed was inevitable, only the order of who sold first, and who sold last, was undetermined.

While it is difficult to say why a white owner moved out, it is safe to say that if they moved to a suburb, their new home would increase in value. It is equally certain that if a black person purchased their home, the home would decrease in value. Their own presence guaranteed it.

As the 1960s rolled along, blockbusting and the white flight it generated snowballed. By the middle of 1965, exactly two years after the first sale, 10% of Evergreen Valley was African American and even black realtors acknowledged it was only a matter of time before African Americans were in the majority. They were right; whites in Evergreen Valley became the minority during the 1970s.[161]

---

[158] *Id.*
[159] *Id.* at 331-334.
[160] *Id.* at 332.
[161] *Id.* at 334.

Whatever the cause, and wherever the blame, in midcentury America, the arrival of the first person of color to a space previously restricted to whites, would usually go one of two ways.

Some communities reacted by attacking the new arrivals with hatred and malice. Often the physical and/or emotional harm inflicted would be sufficient to drive black homebuyers to leave. Even when the initial purchaser withstood the community's venom, the outspoken racism was sufficient to dissuade others from following.[162]

In communities that did not react with acts of hatred or malice, the first arrival often heralded the beginning of a quick, but inevitable process. Seeking to join in a community that welcomed, or at least tolerated racial integration, others would follow. Anxiety would become fear, fear become flight, and flight would become re-segregation. The self-fulfilling prophecy of white flight would again repeat itself.

> "...integration was 'the period between the moving in of the first Negro in a neighborhood and the exit of the last white.'"

As one Flint activist observed in 1963, integration was "the period between the moving in of the first Negro in a neighborhood and the exit of the last white."[163]

Re-segregation was the most insidious result of flight. A leap forward on the path to integration and equal opportunity was quickly followed by dozens of little steps backward until until a person was back at the starting line. It is easy to blame the usual suspects. Most culpable are the realtors who fanned the flames of fear for their own profit. Whites who fled because of their own racism or discomfort were equally blameworthy. It is more difficult to blame whites who fled to protect their own financial interests or to seek better schools for their kids. Many may have stayed, but for their understanding that 'the system' would reward those who left at the expense of those who stayed.

This Commission believes that treating white flight as individual acts of racism is not only too easy, it is counterproductive. Racialized results were created largely by people who were not themselves racists.

Still, whatever the reason for white flight, its existence is built on the legacy of segregation. 'Fleeing' is not caused only by the desire to leave, it requires having somewhere else to go. One could not flee integration if it existed everywhere.

The dirty little secret of white flight is that it was a 'smart' choice. Public policy, or 'the system,' rewarded it. Those who fled were rewarded financially. Their real estate investments increased in value, often supporting them in retirement and providing an inheritance to pass

---

[162] *See, e.g.,* Highsmith at 789; Hammer testimony, Hearing 1 at 35:00.
[163] Highsmith at 333, quoting a statement in the *Flint Journal*, February 8, 1963.

down to the next generation. Those who stayed paid a price. The first sale that 'integrated' a neighborhood systemically and immediately lowered the value of their property, often beginning a cycle in which the longer one waited to sell, the less they would be able to sell for. Flight and re-segregation are not just fueled by individual acts of racists. Systemically created financial rewards and punishments fuel behavior that mimics, and produces and reproduces the same results: spatial segregation.

Consider the residents of Evergreen Valley, but assume that instead of a person of color moving in, a bar had opened. It may have made residents uneasy. The people living closest to it might move, but it would probably not cause 'flight.' However, as more bars opened, more residents would leave, probably for places where bars were not allowed. Residents leaving might even include those who frequented the bars, but also recognized that such establishments were harbingers of neighborhood decline. At some point, even people who liked living close to a bar and still loved their home would be 'smart' to sell it. Those who did not leave would soon find it was too late to sell at a price that would enable them to purchase elsewhere.

When the 'smart' choice is 'coincidentally' the same as the racist's choice, the racism is systemic.

Federal housing policy had treated African Americans as a 'nuisance' in the 1930s and 40s[164] – and while it no longer called them that, it still systemically treated them as such. America had systemically incentivized leaving and punished staying in ways that would encourage *anyone* to leave, *if they could*.

Moreover, the systemic racism that encouraged flight from integration, also encouraged, segregation wherever it still existed. In the real estate parlance of the time, when a black family moved in, the neighborhood became "transitional." Systemically, neighborhoods were not thought of as integrated, they were 'in transition' from all-white to majority black

This reality was recognized, and largely ignored, even as whites fled Flint in the 1950s and 60s. One black realtor in 1965 said about Evergreen Valley that the cycle of integration leading to re-segregation would continue, "unless other neighborhoods in the city become open to Negroes."[165]

Also in 1965, the head of this Commission's Community Relations Division told the Executive Director, "I do not know of even one white community or white section of a city, where a Negro citizen visiting a realtor chosen at random or a home advertised for sale would get the fair and

---

[164] *See* fn 84, supra.
[165] Highsmith at 335.

equitable treatment that is theoretically required by law and this Commission."[166] African American homebuyers would not all have purchased in the same neighborhood had they been able to purchase elsewhere. Black families would have made 'smarter' investments, but were systemically and legally prohibited from doing so. Only white homebuyers had that privilege.

After much talk of the need for "renewal" in downtown Flint, a renewal office opened and the first properties were acquired. This process had barely begun by 1966, but the challenges were apparent. It was a much a greater factor after 1967, but even at the beginning white families had options unavailable to black families. The need for housing continued to grow faster than the ability to break the color lines. But, for most African Americans and especially those who rented, there was no place to go.

6.   The Michigan Civil Rights Commission Hearings of 1966

In 1966, this Commission, prompted by concerns like those noted above and a project by the NAACP and HOME[167] documenting instances of realtors refusing to show properties in white neighborhoods to blacks, held a series of four hearings in Flint devoted to equal housing opportunity.[168] A summary of the hearings, along with Commission findings and recommendations, were later included in a Commission Report. In short, the Commission found that "The City of Flint and the larger metropolitan area are rigidly segregated."[169] Those areas where non-whites were permitted to live were overcrowded, deteriorated, and worsening. The hearings presented a revealing snapshot in time.

a. Segregated

During the course of the Commission hearings, the Director of the Flint Urban League informed Commissioners that the League's most recent national study had determined Flint to be "the most segregated city in the Northeast, North Central, and West regions of the United States." He noted that Flint's segregation index score was 94.4. Fully 94.4% of the African Americans living in the city would have to move elsewhere in order to achieve a "racially balanced residential pattern."

African American brokers were denied membership in the Flint Board of Realtors and could not access the Multiple Listing Exchange, which allowed brokers to learn what houses others had

---

[166] *Id.* at 337, quoting Burton Levy, MCRC Community Relations Division Head, letter to Burton Gordin, Executive Director.

[167] Housing Opportunities Made Equal (HOME) was a local direct action group of Black and white activists working to further fair housing.

[168] The MCRC 1966 hearings were held on November 29 and 30, and December 1 and 9.

[169] 1966 MCRC Report at 14.

for sale. The board also denied black brokers access to the organization's lobbyist, regular meetings with lenders, and the ability to join other organizations or become appraisers.

Commissioners heard testimony that the Board of Realtors had an "unwritten policy" not to sell homes in white neighborhoods to black purchasers, even if the seller wanted them to. The Commission invited Board of Realtors' officers and members to participate in the hearings, and after the first hearing asked for their response, but they declined to participate in the hearings or respond in any way.

Commissioners also heard testimony that brokers and sellers' agents would tell potential customers they would not honor non-discrimination instructions, refused to list homes on a non-discriminatory basis, had a policy not to show or sell a house in a white neighborhood to blacks, and that "it was against their national code of ethics to introduce a foreign element into a neighborhood."

The president of HOME testified that in instances where blacks had been able to move into previously all white areas, "it was necessary for a white person to purchase the house and then resell it to the black purchaser." The black buyers had been told "no" by a realtor before they resorted to the subterfuge. He described how, when he and his wife acted as third-party buyers, a builder told them that to prevent a house from being resold to blacks, the purchase agreement would contain a clause giving the builder an option to void the sale if the original buyer did not occupy the property before it was resold.

> b.   Overcrowded and deteriorated

The Commission's report noted that its members who toured the parts of Flint in which blacks were relegated to live found them to be "clustered around industrial complexes and contained what appeared to be a high proportion of substandard housing." According to 1960 census figures, 21% of the city's housing units were substandard.

According to the Urban League Housing Committee report, the census tracts with the highest proportion of substandard housing were those with the highest non-white population ratios. The 1966 report quoted a Fire Department official as saying: "Our records indicate virtually no rental vacancies of residential housing that will pass code standards."

A black businesswoman and longtime resident of northeast Flint complained of industrial smog. She described how caustic deposits from the smokestacks of a nearby foundry were causing damage to property. She said a public health official told her the area had the city's highest incidence of cancer. She then noted (in testimony eerily similar to what we heard during our hearings) that both she and her husband had suffered from throat cancer. She had undergone surgery, but his already killed him.

A Genesee County Bureau of Social Aid caseworker reported that 30 of the 70 families assigned to her lived in "obviously substandard" houses (four actually condemned), but owners wouldn't repair them because it was easier to evict tenants and find others. She said 33 of the 70 lived in overcrowded conditions including one or two family houses converted to hold five to seven families.

Families reported that available housing was overcrowded, unsafe, or unsanitary. They said landlords didn't comply with code enforcement orders, and some evicted tenants who complained.

A representative of the Michigan Catholic Conference described how many landlords deliberately exploited the situation. He said when his next door neighbors, one of three white families in one house, asked the landlord to improve the property, the landlord told them that if they complained too much about the conditions, he would evict them and "put n*****s in the house" because he "could get more money per week out of the house if he had n*****s in it anyway, and the n*****s wouldn't complain because they have no place to stay."

c. Worsening

In the late 1960s, worsening conditions were not only caused by the continuing influx of people into the same defined amount of space, but also because the space was beginning to shrink due to the introduction of what was promised to be "renewal."

Flint's Mayor told the Commission that over 3,000 families had been or would be displaced by highway and urban renewal activities in Flint. The Director of the Central Relocation Office estimated that approximately 2,400 families would be dislocated by the highway project alone, adding that all of these families would have to move within the next 13 months. Over one-half of the families were African American, meaning that an average of 100 black families would need new housing each month.

The Relocation Director further noted that 85% of the families were low income, over half qualified for public housing, many received social aid, and one quarter had senior citizens as heads of the household.

But as to the availability of adequate housing to meet the needs of the dislocated, the Mayor testified that 192 units of public housing would be available early in 1967, and that the city was

working on a plan to acquire and rehabilitate large houses to accommodate families too large for the public housing units under construction. Other than these projects and the existence of a few FHA 22I(d)3 developments,[170] he admitted the Flint area presented a "dismal low-rent housing picture." The Urban League Director said of the relocation problem: "This city is really in deep trouble on this score. ... I don't see the housing and I don't see it on the drawing boards."

Spokesmen for the Genesee County Development Conference explained, somewhat incongruously, that they had postponed development of low and moderate income housing due to the more pressing demand imposed by assuming operation of the highway relocation program.

The Relocation Office Director testified that his staff had used every available means to assist such families, but added that decent and affordable rental facilities were practically non-existent, characterizing Flint's rental housing market as "vicious." The Supervisor of the Genesee County Bureau of Social Aid explained: "If one is classified as a Welfare recipient, it is almost impossible to rent or make a purchase of a home. If you are a member of a racial minority group… and a welfare recipient, locating housing then becomes a real problem."

Asked about the equality of housing opportunities for white and non-white displaced families, the Relocation Director pointed out that his office would only promote a home if it could be shown on a non-discriminatory basis. He also conceded that as a result, the properties posted on their bulletin board tended to be only those in black and integrated neighborhoods. He pointed out that this also limited the houses office could offer to Caucasians, and that "[a]s a result, most people seeking sales property turn to other sources." Because they were the only ones who were permitted to buy from the other sources, "most people" was code for "most whites." He said that on 16 of 156 confirmed moves to date were black families, and all moved into neighborhoods with mixed or black populations. Almost all the other families had moved into predominantly white neighborhoods, adding that "Caucasians, have been much freer . . . in their movement as to where they have gone."

d. Real people

Interestingly, the 1966 hearings also painted a more personal picture of what segregation looked like through the eyes of Flint's residents. Imagine being:

- The African American whose employment by a federal agency required him to transfer to Flint and who described the difficulty he had trying to find a place to rent. He said he was asked about his skin color when he called a rental agent to inquire about vacancies. He was told by a real estate broker that he couldn't rent an available apartment in a white apartment building, and eventually bought a home in a "racially changing area."

---

[170] Section 221(d)(4) insures mortgage loans to facilitate the new construction or substantial rehabilitation of multifamily rental or cooperative housing for moderate-income families, elderly, and the handicapped. 24 USC 221(d)(4).

- Another transferred federal employee described how he ran into two different patterns of discrimination while trying to find a place to live. In smaller buildings he found that after he would inquire by phone, "vacancies would disappear" by the time he arrived to visit to the building. Larger buildings, he said, would take his application and the "forget about it." In other words, this happened often enough for him to detect trends. (The Report notes a pharmacist related similar experiences.)

- The clergyman's wife who explained that after she and her husband had approached several real estate brokers, they ultimately could only obtain a house they wanted by having a white third party buyer purchase it for them and resell it to them.

- The two newly hired teachers who, according to a member of the Flint Human Relations Commission, were ultimately forced to cancel their contracts with Flint schools, because their race made it impossible for them to secure adequate housing.

- A number of home-seekers shared stories about how realtors refused to show them houses unless the neighborhood was black, or already transitioning.

Or imagine being one of these residents, and while waiting to testify, hearing:

- The Superintendent of Flint's "Community Schools," who admitted that only 10-15% of the city's schools had racial compositions that "approached" the population of the system as a whole. But then blamed the "degree of racial imbalance" on "long established patterns of housing segregation in the City of Flint." He did so without explaining why students were assigned to schools not closest to their houses, how blacks and whites living on the same street could be going to different schools, or why black students were assigned to overcrowded schools further away from their homes, instead of the closer all-white school that was below capacity.

- Genesee County Board of Supervisors' Legislative Committee Chairman, who admitted "equal housing opportunities do not today exist in Genesee County," but contended it was primarily due to self-segregation by African Americans, economic factors, and white resistance to integration.

In December 1966, the Michigan Civil Rights Commission found Flint to be just as segregated as it had been at the end of the Great Depression, with housing hardly in any better shape than it had been at that time.

They found African Americans "rigidly segregated" and "concentrated in contiguous census tracts in the inner core of the city." These areas had "a high proportion of substandard housing and tend[ed] to be clustered around industrial complexes." The Commission further found families displaced primarily by freeway projects that were in "severe hardship" and in need of housing, but "no indications that an adequate supply of such housing in standard condition, either public or private, now exists or will be available." The lack of housing was "compounded by the prevailing pattern of housing discrimination and segregation," and by the "large amount of housing in Flint that is not fit for human habitation."

7. Rebellion and Aftermath

There has been great debate about what to call the 1967 civil disturbances in Detroit and Flint. The terms most often used, "riot" and "rebellion," are both factually and grammatically correct. The term riot suggests property destruction and violence being committed by uncontrolled mobs of hooligans, thugs and lawbreakers for no reason other than the lack of anything better to do. Rebellion, on the other hand, suggests a more organized group taking actions calculated to bring about desired change. What took place in 1967 was certainly both depending upon the viewpoint one takes. In the African American community, the 1967 civil disturbances are often referred to as the "rebellion" while others refer to these disturbances as the "riot."

We choose to use the term rebellion because we believe what took place was more a reaction than action. We believe that if any lesson is to be learned from these events, it is that (at least in the eyes of those who participated) they were in response to, and defiance of, government control and authority.

While similar to rebellions in other cities, the rebellion in Flint was different in one respect. The rebellion in Flint was not only predictable, it was predicted. In fact, Flint's rebellion resulted in comparatively light damage due in part to African Americans in Flint being restricted to the same limited sections of an urban core despite the growth in their numbers.

Most Americans had recognized the evil of segregation and were at least beginning to dismantle it. In Flint, however, the city government and particularly the schools claimed they could do nothing about segregation because it was caused by individuals.

The 1967 rebellion in Flint was about fair housing. More accurately, it was about the lack of fair housing and the lack of fair housing laws. Flint's City Council refused to pass a fair housing law saying that the owner of a piece of property had no right to dictate the skin color of the people next door, and the seller of property had no right to dictate the skin color of the people who would live there after they moved away.

Following the 1966 hearings, this Commission's opening recommendation to the "city officials of Flint" could not have been clearer: "Enact a comprehensive ordinance prohibiting discrimination in housing." The issue over a fair housing ordinance became the most discussed issue in Flint, dominating press headlines and Council meeting agendas. But meeting after meeting, the Council found some reason to postpone voting on the issue.[171]

At its July 17, 1967 meeting, a concerned citizen advised the Flint City Council:

> Most Negroes as well as other minority groups are concentrated in old inferior housing in old inferior neighborhoods. Many of these dwellings are unfit for human habitation, but these citizens have little if any alternative and are forced to pay exorbitant rates for dilapidated, roach and rat infested facilities. . . . The past practices of the Federal government, the past and current policies and practices of real estate agencies and commercial home builders and the racial fears of white homeowners—which have been exploited by the opponents of fair housing programs have all contributed to a situation which is a disgraceful affront to our common democratic heritage. . . . We have long since learned that the deadliest factor mitigating against desegregation—particularly in housing is equivocation on the part of authority figures at the top. Unless elected officials take a firm and positive stand [on open occupancy], dissident elements come to believe that their only rewarding means of protest is open violence and rebellion. Under these circumstances, it is guaranteed that they are going to rebel against life in the ghetto. . . .[172]

Exactly one week later, "dissident elements" did.

On the evening of July 24, a day after the start of the Detroit rebellion, hundreds of protesters gathered on Flint's North End. After the protest broke up, a much smaller group of people turned to violence, burning some 17 structures, throwing stones at passing cars and shop windows, and looting some stores.[173] Within 24 hours, Governor Romney declared a state of emergency in the area, set up state police roadblocks, banned the carrying of weapons, closed gas stations and banned sales of alcohol. Members of local African American civil rights groups took to the streets to quiet tensions and restore order. By July 27, Flint's rebellion was over.[174]

However, the fight for equal housing would continue. As the rebellion wound down, activists (both black and white) attended a city council meeting on July 27 to demand passage of an already watered down open housing ordinance. The vote took place on August 14; three

---

[171] Highsmith, *supra* at 348-350.

[172] *Id.* at 350, quoting Marise Hadden address to Flint City Commission, July 17, 1967.

[173] *Id.* at 350-353.

[174] *Id.*

council members voted for, five against. The housing ordinance was defeated.[175] Nothing had changed.

E. 1968-2010: Good Intentions, Bad Results

1. Fair Housing Isn't

Coming just weeks after the rebellion, the city council's August 14 rejection of what advocates believed was a weak fair housing ordinance (calling for "open housing") brought immediate condemnation. Before the meeting had ended, Mayor Floyd J. McCree, Flint's first African American Mayor, stated "I'm not going to sit up here any longer and live an equal opportunity lie" and resigned.

In the week following the Mayor's resignation the city witnessed: similar resignations by dozens of city officials and appointees (both black and white); a continuing 'sleep-in' protest on the city hall lawn; and a "Unity Rally" that was the largest protest gathering Flint had ever seen. The rally not only brought thousands of protesters, but both Governor George Romney and Attorney General Frank Kelley also attended. These events brought national and international attention to Flint's refusal to adopt fair housing, including a ten-minute segment on national (Huntly-Brinkley) television news.[176]

With the protest in, and attention on, Flint, many civic groups and some elected officials changed their positions. Before the end of October Mayor McCree was back in place and the council narrowly adopted an (even more watered down) open housing ordinance by a vote of five to four.[177]

The adoption of the ordinance was immediately met with a public petition drive to annul it. Although successful in getting the matter on the ballot, opponents of open housing narrowly lost at the polls. The vote favoring open housing was praised widely as a victory for all the people of Flint, but a great majority of whites voted against it. The campaign had been so brutal that a step in the direction of integration also increased the resistance to it, and widened the racial divide confronted by African Americans within Flint.[178]

Even after adoption of the Fair Housing Act in 1968, making open housing the law nationally, the 1970s saw the phenomenon of white flight skyrocket. Fifty years of official government

---

[175] *Id.* at 353.
[176] *Id.* at 354-356.
[177] *Id.* at 359-361.
[178] *Id.*

policy, practical experience, and real estate history, were deeply embedded. The Flint versus suburbs mentality and decades of discrimination and racial inequality had erected an invisible but very real "racial divide." Everyone "knew" that a property's value would go down with every black family that moved into the neighborhood. For many, if not most, homeowners, it did not matter why this was true, it was simply accepted as a fact.

Blockbusting, unscrupulous realtors, mortgage redlining, and racist whites, all continued to play their role in white flight, but once again flight was often motivated by personal opportunity, not animus. Race had been so ingrained into the system that individual whites need not act out of animus in order for blacks to experience it. Again, not all sellers were motivated by the color of their new neighbors' skin. Many simply wanted to sell as quickly as possible before the value further deteriorated and moved because it was the "smart" financial decision.

However, even if much of the continuing flight to the suburbs in the 1970s and beyond can be explained as economic flight rather than white flight, seeing events through this lens ignores several critical facts:

First, it ignores the reality that because of racial restrictions, only whites *could* move to the suburbs. It is pointless to contend that black families should have seen the same economic forces at play and left the city in search of greener pastures like whites did because suburban home ownership was universally restricted to whites only.

Second, it underlines the insidious nature of systemic racism – by simply buying a home, a person of color would drive that property's value down from what was paid. Thus, the economic benefit of investing in home ownership was denied to people of color.

Black families were not only prevented by deed restrictions from making good real estate investments, they were forced to make bad ones by purchasing homes that would decrease in value even as they continued to make mortgage payments. Black families that were prevented from purchasing a home were forced to pay rent (at rates driven up by high demand and low supply) and unable to build wealth through home ownership. Many white families are financially where they are today in large part due to investments in home ownership made at a time when the same economic opportunity was denied to African American families.

And the harm was not only directly to the opportunity to build wealth. The spatial concentration that resulted from denying these economic opportunities to African Americans, also created economic realities that prevented the kind of investment in public schools and municipal infrastructure necessary to keep up with the suburbs being created by those who benefited from them. This in turn led to lower educational outcomes for black children.

Even the problem with the water distribution system relates directly to flight. Today's crisis involves a water plant and system designed to move water for twice the current population. The loss of industrial facilities only exacerbated the "spatial mismatch" created by the population loss. The result is a poor, less educated and disproportionately black population left behind with a shrinking tax base and a greater share of the city's costs (including costs related to the sprawl of others). To compound the problem, rather than assist with these costs, the State significantly reduced its revenue sharing[179], further aggravating the city's economic woes.

Finally, while 'economic flight' might explain the actions of many of the whites who left the city, the desire to make good financial decisions cannot explain the numbers of vacant houses.[180] During the 1970s thousands left for new suburban homes without being able to sell their old ones. In 1979, almost 10% of Flint homes (20% in some areas) were unoccupied.[181] These people were *not* motivated by investment opportunity.

2. Renewal Without Renewal is Destruction

Urban renewal sounded promising, but in the end it was yet another contributor to Flint's urban despair. The idea was to build new economic engines on land occupied by those who were least well off, allowing them to move to better housing in better neighborhoods. As implemented, it had two fatal flaws. First, due to bad decisions (Auto World) and poor projections of need (I-475), the renewal projects would create little, if any, economic benefit. Equally harmful, the displacement of residents took place with little regard for where they could go.

Urban renewal discussion and planning began in Flint as early as the 1950s, as GM was decentralizing its manufacturing and saw the advantages and cost savings that easy freeway access to plants offered both the company and its employees. In 1963, the state formally joined the effort when the Michigan State Highway Department (MSHD) issued a planning report entitled "Freeways for Flint."[182]

MSHD proposed a north/south highway (I-475) and an east/west connector (then M-78, now I-69), which, along with an interchange, would be built over what was the St. John neighborhood. The selection of the location was no accident. It was chosen based on an analysis that included not only its proximity to downtown, but also factors like lower property taxes, lower property values (acquisition costs), and higher level of impoverishment. [183] No mention was made of St.

---

[179] Sadler at 7. Between 2003 and 2014, Flint lost $54.9 million.

[180] *See, e.g.,* Highsmith at 416, 554.

[181] *Id.* at 498.

[182] *Id.* 412, 441-443.

[183] *Id.* at 413.

John's central role in the lives of African Americans. Largely prohibited elsewhere it was where blacks shopped, ate, had their hair done/cut, and found entertainment.

The anticipated urban renewal efforts were initially supported by African American residents and activists. [184] They saw the promises of renewal and open housing working together to provide real change and improvement in peoples' living conditions while also integrating housing. However, this support started dissipating once implementation started.[185]

Renewal relocations failed to produce significant improvement in living conditions; often it did precisely the opposite. Actual property acquisition and relocation efforts to make for renewal did not began until 1965. They were first suspended in 1967 due to federal budget cuts necessary to fund the Vietnam war, and proceeded sporadically until the last piece of property was purchased in 1977.[186] The efforts were consistently hindered by the lack of affordable and available alternate housing for those being displaced.

In addition to the old problems of mortgages and racial exclusions, a number of new government-created problems made the relocation experience of blacks even more difficult and inequitable. The decision to reimburse based on fair market value of their homes rather than the costs of relocating, was particularly harmful since residents often had invested substantially in their properties even though the homes had depressed values.[187] To make matters even worse, every delay caused home prices to dip even further.

From the moment the city announced its intention to purchase and redevelop the land in 1958, everyone knew which areas were slated for condemnation. In 1965, to keep eventual purchase costs low, the city council passed an ordinance prohibiting all but ordinary maintenance on homes. Unable to do anything else, homeowners had to watch their property and property value decline. As a result, many homeowners were forced to relocate to public housing. Businesses were similarly not paid enough for their properties to allow them to open elsewhere.[188]

Renewal relocations also failed to produce significant housing integration. Displaced black families were limited in their choices, and prevented from considering the suburbs. The few instances where blacks broke the color-line, were soon nullified by flight and re-segregation.

---

[184] *Id.* at 416-418, 429-431.
[185] *Id.* 434-437.
[186] *Id.* 455-459, 464.
[187] *Id.* at 459.
[188] *Id.* at 458-465

Public housing policies also directly contributed to preserving segregation. The federal government's Section 235 program subsidized construction of roughly 1,250 public housing homes between 1968 and 1970 alone. The homes were however lacking in two key measures: quality and location.

In 1970, Governor Romney, who had been appointed to serve as U.S. Secretary of Housing and Urban Development, launched an effort to combat the segregation partially created by FHA mortgages by erecting public housing in suburban locations. Unfortunately, these homes were often poorly constructed and nearly all purchasers found problems with their new homes, including safety and building code violations. A 1974 study by the Genesee County Metropolitan Planning Commission found 83% of the homes reporting construction related defects, with fully two-thirds of all units beset by plumbing problems. The required repairs were made in less than 20% of the homes. More than a quarter of the new owners left their homes by the end of 1974, many due to the recession, but often as a result of bankruptcies caused by repair costs, often within months of occupancy.[189]

Nor was the public housing built in white suburban neighborhoods. Nearly two-thirds was built within the city. The others were constructed in small clusters, mostly just north of the city limits in the unincorporated Beecher Metropolitan District which already had black residents. Clustering the low income housing only in already integrated neighborhoods had the immediate effect of accelerating fear, blockbusting, and flight. Integrated neighborhoods became re-segregated because segregated white communities were permitted to stay that way.[190]

The same slow destruction without renewal was simultaneously taking place in Floral Park. While the projects were different, the pattern of destruction was the same.

In the end urban renewal caused more harm than good. Flint's vibrant African American communities had been razed, the good along with the deteriorated and overcrowded. The existing urban culture was erased. In its place are freeways, a theme park, and other underused facilities that, like Flint's water system, were built for people and businesses who largely are no longer there.

Unless ALL communities are open, some communities get more of what or whoever others keep out. No matter what the perceived "problem" is, if it is shared equally it does not affect relative housing prices/value. Historically, building low income housing in one community lowers property values because it is not happening everywhere else. Adding more public housing near existing public housing ensures neighboring property values decline, even as values go up and 'reward' those in neighborhoods that block such housing.

---

[189] *Id.* at 507-510, 516.
[190] *Id.* at 518-519.

Because the land is cheap and opposition limited, the system silently works to ensure programs like public housing (or environmental risks) end up being placed in the least affluent communities. It is not just those living in the public housing who suffer the consequences, it is the entire community. Permitting public housing to be treated like an undesirable public nuisance and placing it where resistance is lowest, also ensures it will be kept out of communities where resources like schools are sufficient to support it.

This is also how many whites become victims of racism. Although government officially stopped treating African Americans like a "nuisance" as it had decades earlier,[191] the system continued to do exactly that. Everyone's property value goes down, and soon people are financially 'trapped' in those homes.

F. Housing and schools

This Commission did not identify Flint schools as a separate topic during the 2016 hearings, and thus will not address it here in great detail. However, the Flint of today cannot be understood without recognizing that the history of Flint school policies, and often the explicit actions of its school board, played a significant role in protecting the spatial segregation of Flint's housing. It also played a key role in shaping race relations, both in the way schools themselves treated it, and by creating community identity around schools in ways that prevented black and white residents from interacting socially.

Flint schools have a history that is typical of other urban districts, and yet unique to Flint. These will be briefly reviewed separately, though they overlap in both time and impact.

1. Neighborhood-centered community schools

The involvement of Charles Stewart Mott and the Foundation that bore his name made Flint schools unique. Mott himself made his fortune in the automobile business, first manufacturing wheels for bicycles and carriages, then switching to doing so for automobiles in Utica, New York, and then in Flint, after reaching a major deal with Billy Durant and Buick Motors. He then sold his operations to General Motors and joined its Board as a major stockholder. He was a capitalist's capitalist.[192]

His first political experience came in 1912 when, after helping form the "Independent Citizens Party" in response to victories by Flint's Socialist Party, he was elected as Flint's Mayor. Mott

---

[191] See fn 84.
[192] Highsmith at 96-98.

would later serve additional one-year terms beginning in 1913 and 1918. In 1920, he unsuccessfully ran for Governor.[193]

Mott's nemesis was what we would now call 'big government.' He viewed progressive taxation and similar "redistributive liberalism" as "creeping socialism" and instead favored self-help initiatives to direct assistance, particularly when government was involved.[194] He fought against everything the "New Deal" stood for.

In addition to ushering the New Deal programs, the Great Depression had left Flint schools and industry in desperate conditions. In 1935, Mott funded a limited plan to test the idea of turning schools into recreation centers after school hours. This first limited program had similarly limited aims: combat juvenile delinquency and promote child safety. It was very successful.[195]

Then came the "Sit-Down Strikes" of 1936-1937. As a result of the strikes, GM recognized and entered into collective bargaining with the newly formed United Auto Workers union. The organization drives by labor that the Sit-Downers both represented and helped launch, did not sit well with Mott. The neighborhood-based community education programs he created thereafter were seen by many as his response to this movement.[196]

The recreation program grew, both in size and scope. During 1937 Mott increased funding by nearly 500%, and turned his attention to the non-recreational needs of the families it was serving in its 22 operating school centers. During WWII, it expanded to include a health center as well as programs for vocational training, homemaking for adult women, and domestic training for new mothers. The latter two programs were intended to directly address the often unsatisfactory living arrangements of working class Catholics, and the unfamiliar child-rearing, worship, cooking, cleaning, and other social practices of immigrants.[197]

In 1947, Mott launched the Fairview Project which represented a significant evolution in his approach. Until then, all of the schools with which Mott had worked had been white. He experimented with the "Flint Interracial Community Center" beginning in 1945 fearing racial violence like the riot that had taken place in Detroit two years earlier, but the name was a misnomer. While billed as an effort to improve conditions "between the races," the center's location in the St. John neighborhood assured that actual racial interaction would be between the black and Mexican residents who lived there. The new project was also in St. John, but

---

[193] *Id.* at 98-99.
[194] *Id.* at 102, 127-128.
[195] *Id.* at 103-106.
[196] *Id.* at 106-107.
[197] *Id.* at 110-111.

while Fairview School was only a short distance away from the "Interracial" center, it dropped any such pretense.

The Fairview Project was structured to improve people's lives, and in this way was benevolent, but only to a point. The Mott Foundation designed the Fairview Project specifically to "lessen frustration and aggression" of St. John residents. It had no illusions of integrating blacks into white society or providing them equal opportunity. It was intent on keeping them separate, but making them less frustrated about it. The Project was built upon the premise that two types of families lived in St. John: "In the Fairview District, the serious-minded parents who want better things for their children find life a continuous struggle to combat destructive influences. Children whose parents have long since bowed to prevailing conditions come to school in a poor state of nutrition and health, with serious behavior problems and little hope for the future."[198]

In the words of its chief architect: "[The project] doesn't mean that the races have to date or inter-marry . . . [but] we should put the Negro on our middle class level of thinking. We have to take out the good Negro and bring him along to our middle class."[199]

It tried to accomplish its goal by using the school setting as the center for all community activity, not only for the school day itself, but also for all other community needs, including public health, child care, recreation, adult programming (including homemaking courses to teach mothers to cook, clean, and sew), meeting space and recreational opportunities for all ages.[200]

As part of the Fairview Project, the Mott Foundation also reviewed and made numerous changes to the school's curriculum. This included stronger academics and longer class periods, as well as an orchestra, field trips, intense physical education, and regular intelligence and achievement testing. All tailored to meet (what the Foundation and School Board determined to be) the specific needs of the neighborhood.[201]

The Fairview Project was a huge success. Although little or no effort was made to determine whether the Project improved educational, employment or health outcomes for students or community members, it kept them very busy. The influx of capital from Mott at a time when

---

[198] *Id.* at 114.

[199] *Id.* quoting Frank Manley, described as the founder of community schools. He was a Mott Foundation trustee and acted as its spokesperson on the subject.

[200] *Id.* at 114-118.

[201] *Id.*

the school system as a whole was still suffering from the depression and a lack of funds, made Fairview a model school, a hub for adult education, and a busy community center – all carefully customized to the neighborhood it anchored. The Project's success story (with the help of the Foundation's publicity efforts) drew the attention of the entire city, and was soon the mold by which all Flint schools were shaped.[202]

Building on the Fairview Project model, the Mott Foundation set its sights on expanding its reach. In 1950, Charles Mott announced that he would donate $1 million for construction of a four-year college in Flint, conditioned upon Flint voters passing a $7 million public school millage. When the millage passed, the Mott-friendly school board began constructing new schools and converting the entire system into community based schools.[203]

By 1960, the school board had built eight new elementary community schools/centers. Seven were in the all-white suburban ring on the city's outer edge. The only one with any students of color, the eighth school, was 83% black. Throughout this period and until at least 1970, Mott's community schools approach was Flint's educational guiding star. The neighborhood school was the center of all activity, and served the needs of the community. Education and curricula were tailored to fit the needs of the community being served. This fit well with Mott's own philosophy that the common interest was served by sorting and separating students by race, space, and class.[204]

In the 1960s, it was impossible to determine where the Mott program ended and public schools began. The Mott community schools did not create the spatial separation that reflected race and class in Flint – but they did institutionalize it. School district lines no longer merely defined where children went to school; they now also dictated what the student could learn. They also defined the social sphere of life. Nearly all of one's activities outside work took place with the people who lived in the same space as you did, and the activities were largely what others believed people like you should want. Race defined where you lived, and where you lived defined everything else.

At the same time, the school board adopted ostensibly race neutral (colorblind) standards to separate students by ability level, and tailored the education they received accordingly. Using the "primary cycle" and "Strawman Procedure on Grouping," students were assessed, placed

---

[202] *Id.*
[203] *Id.* at 117-119.
[204] *Id.* at 117-119, 93.

and educated based upon their 'ability' as determined by classroom performance, achievement tests, and intelligence quotient measurements.[205]

Basing curricula on student 'ability' not only dictated that segregated schools had different programs intended to produce different results, it also had the effect of racially segregating students within the few schools where students of different races were accepted. The system's Personalized Curriculum Program identified which students would be placed into programs intended for the "Talented Child" verses those intended to provide a "Better Tomorrow for the Urban Youth."[206]

The significance of such sorting was apparent to all. Schools with black majorities had vocational and life skills curricula aimed at providing a "Better Tomorrow." The Foundation and school board had created a system that, while ostensibly tailored to meet each student and community's needs, also dictated the future for which the student was being prepared. As one former Flint student put it: "Most black folks they put on the track system. They'd train you to be able to go into General Motors but not to be able to go to college. That's the kind of system they had you on, taking home economics and gym."[207]

Similarly, adult classes were intended "to improve the cultural and intellectual life of the community, to increase citizens' knowledge of their economy, home roles and heritage, and to meet the special needs of the people."[208]

Mott's community schools were unabashed in their aims. Mott Foundation Trustee Frank Manley, described as the founder of community schools, explained that when appropriate, community schools should set aside "intellectualism" in favor of "life skills." As he saw it, "Educators these days are concentrating on geniuses, but we're more interested in the *hoi polloi* . . . so we're promoting education for people who haven't had the opportunity to learn."[209]

The Foundation's ultimate interest was not education for educations sake. Education, and Mott-styled community schools in particular, was seen as a tool for solving all the world's ills.

---

[205] *Id.* at 170-172.

[206] *Id.*

[207] *Id.* at 171, quote attributed to former Flint City Councilman Woody Etherly, Jr., Northern High class of 1962; citing Rhonda Sanders, *Bronze Pillars: An Oral History of African-Americans in Flint* (1995).

[208] *Id.* at 123 quoting a leaflet titled "Divisions of the Mott Program of the Flint Board of Education."

[209] *Id.* at 124.

Manley believed that if "by some magic" all schools would follow his community school model, "human suffering and despair could be virtually be eliminated from the face of the earth."[210] However, this noble goal, and thus the programing of their community schools, was premised on Charles Mott's personal philosophy (which was ideally suited for a place as segregated as Flint). It envisioned races getting along and working together, by living apart, and individuals participating in ways 'appropriate' to one's race and standing. Its supporters felt the New Deal and other such liberal programs rewarded laziness, and that this lack of work ethic was the reason some people (individuals or races) were less well off than others.

The view was that community education would not redistribute wealth as liberals and socialists urged, it would make people earn it. Rather than reward people for being lazy, it would teach them to take personal responsibility for fulfilling their own needs. Solving poverty meant reforming the attitudes and behaviors of poor people. If someone was unemployed it was because they didn't want to work, not because there were no jobs. Hunger was the fault of "mothers who are too dilatory or too indolent to get up in the morning to prepare breakfast for their children."[211] To understand the futility of this simplistic approach, one need only visualize what it would look like if a person literally attempted to lift themselves up by pulling on their own bootstraps (or shoelaces).

Housing segregation, by this reasoning, was similar in nature to the schools' Personalized Curriculum Program. It was not discriminatory, it just reflected that people who were alike benefit from being grouped together. The "racial divide" by this reasoning, merely put people where they belonged.

Because "human suffering and despair" were the fault of those suffering – they would go away if people simply became good workers, content in the role and place they were destined for.

Community education would train them to do just that.

2. Separate and unequal, northern style school segregation

While the relationship between the Mott Foundation and the public school system may have been unique, the way Flint School Board's members(often Mott-backed) preserved school segregation was more typical. District boundaries were simply changed to mirror racial movement.

Ironically, the first instance of gerrymandering school district lines occurred in 1935, just as Charles Mott expressed interest in creating recreational programs centered in schools. It

---

[210] *Id.* at 127, citing W. Fred Totten and Frank Manley, "The Community School: Basic Concepts, Function, and Organization" (Galien, Michigan: Allied Education Council, 1969).
[211] *Id.* at 128, quoting "The Community School," *supra.*

happened quietly and without fanfare. After the families of a few black students formerly living in the still integrated Parkland school district purchased property in the all-white Dort school district, some locals expressed concern. In response, the school board moved the border between the districts one block south. This returned 100% of Dort's black students back to Parkland and the 'problem' was corrected.[212]

With this one exception, no other district gerrymandering occurred until the 1950s. Deeply entrenched spatial segregation in housing made it unnecessary. That changed overall and particularly among blacks as Flint's population grew after WWII, and after the 1950 millage provided the school board funds to build new schools. One early example was Pierce School which opened in 1952 and was one of the first buildings constructed with the millage funding. Pierce School was built to take the pressure off the overcrowded and deteriorating Clark School. It was erected in a subdivision of newly constructed homes with FHA supported mortgages, *i.e.*, it was 100% white.[213]

Although policy specified that students be assigned to the school closest to them, they weren't.

Pierce opened with an all-white student body. It was also under capacity and remained that way for the rest of the decade. At the same time, Clark remained overcrowded and almost all black, even though many of its black students lived closer to the unfilled Pierce. The school board explained the situation by saying the new district line was based on a small stream that formed the district's jagged southwestern edge. The stream, it so happened was also the demarcation line between two spatially segregated neighborhoods.[214]

If the school board's use of the small stream to avoid its own proximity rule left any doubt about the board's actual intent, it was short lived. After learning where the district line had been drawn, parents on the 'wrong' side of the stream began requesting transfers to the closer, newer, and under-capacity Pierce school. Without providing any explanation, the board denied all requests filed on behalf of black students, while granting requests from white families.[215]

Pierce remained all-white and under capacity while nearly 300 black students attended school in temporary classrooms located in old rundown houses, while waiting for yet another new school to relieve overcrowding at Clark. When the Stewart School opened, the board again redrew district lines with little regard for its professed proximity rule. This time the irregular lines were drawn so that the white students remaining in Clark were transferred to Pierce as

---

[212] *Id.* at 151-152.
[213] *Id.* at 155-157.
[214] *Id.*
[215] *Id.*

possible, while all black students moved to Stewart, which was already 80% black when it opened in 1955.

At the beginning of the 1960s, Pierce was 100% white and still under capacity while Clark remained over capacity and 99.5% black. As for boundary lines between the districts: "They drew boundaries around houses, down the middle of the street. . .. When blacks moved onto a street, they would change the boundaries."[216] Students on the same street were assigned schools by race, not location.

Building new schools to house additional students also created other issues. As the schools were built, and sometimes as they opened, the board faced *awkward* situations that necessitated sending a group of black students to a white school, or more often, where *new* white families closer to an all-white school necessitated moving *current* white students from the all-white schools they had been attending to relieve overcrowding. The board responded to these scenarios by developing "primary units."[217]

Primary units were essentially ranch houses built to serve as temporary school and then sold as residential homes when no longer needed. Over 100 such units were used over the 15 years they were deployed. They were most often found in newer areas where new families were moving into new housing, and accordingly used for only white students.[218]

Examples of the lengths the board went to preserve racial hegemony were not difficult to find. In 1964, many families were forced to relocate to make room for freeways as the city's 'renewal' efforts began. Lewis and Fairview schools were only a mile from each other, but they couldn't look any different. Lewis had a capacity of 661 and an enrollment of 892 students, while Fairview school had a capacity of 445, but an enrollment of only 305 students. Why such a difference? Fairview had five black students, while Lewis had four white students.

Those few black students who attended virtually all-white schools faced a different form of segregation. In Homedale elementary, which had 830 students in 1959, of whom only 11 were black, complaints from white parents caused a second grade teacher to separate the one black student in her classroom from the 29 white students – by having him sit in a small closet.[219]

---

[216] *Id.* at 157, quoting resident Ruth Scott, citing R. Sanders, *Bronze Pillars*.
[217] Highsmith at 160-166.
[218] *Id.*
[219] *Id.* at 169.

The 1954 landmark U. S. Supreme Court decision *Brown v Board of Education*[220] did little to change anything in Flint, despite famously proclaiming that "in the field of public education, the doctrine of "separate but equal" has no place."[221] Black students were not to be excluded from white schools, even if the National Guard had to be called in. So why then, was there no interruption in the segregation of Flint's students?

In simple terms, Flint did not have *white* schools, it had *neighborhood* schools where students were assigned to schools based on their addresses. *Brown* prohibited the government from discriminating based on race, but said nothing about 'race neutral' or 'colorblind' government policies that separated students based on their address and 'merely' resulted in racial segregation. In the parlance of the day, *Brown* prohibited only *de jure* (in law) discrimination, not *de facto* (in practice) discrimination.

Thus, when the Flint Urban League examined Flint's all black schools shortly after the Brown decision and asked the question, "Is this because of segregation in the public schools?" Its answer was "No." The Urban League explained, "Flint is at the top of the list noticeably in the degree of neighborhood segregation. Each public school is organized to serve its immediate neighborhood. As the direct result of neighborhood segregation, some Flint schools inevitably are segregated."[222]

In Flint, community schools didn't segregate the neighborhoods, the neighborhoods segregated community schools. Even the fact that school district lines weren't actually being drawn based on proximity seemed unimportant because they were still being drawn around houses not people.

Using the concept of *de facto* discrimination as an explanation for government actions was again front and center in the late 1970s, when Flint faced the prospect of judicially imposed integration and the Mott Foundation stepped away from Flint's community schools. This Commission believes the concept of *de facto* discrimination is key in understanding what is taking place in Flint today.

3. A word about Mott

There is no question that Charles S. Mott and the Mott Foundation played an outsized role in keeping Flint's schools segregated, and in "tracking" African Americans on paths that did not include college. Further, the spatial segregation that characterized Flint's housing and the

---

[220] *Brown v. Board of Education of Topeka*, 347 U.S. 483 (1954).
[221] *Id.* at 495.
[222] *Id.* at 369, quoting William S. Price, III, "Implications in U.S. Supreme Court Ruling on Segregation in Public Schools," [ca. 1955].

segregation of Flint's schools are so intertwined that the Mott community schools program not only reflected the spatial racism, it contributed greatly to preserving it.

It would be easy to point the finger at the Mott Foundation and blame it for Flint's segregated schools, and for the unequal education they dispensed. The consequences from well-intended people and programs nevertheless contributed to spatial segregation in Flint. Structuring educational opportunity that took into account race has long abandoned, but it still leaves "deep scars" that is part of the legacy of Flint.

We find that white students' needs were almost always addressed first, including placement in the newer and better schools, while all but a very few black students were denied access to programs that would open the door to higher education and greater opportunity. These are facts, and they constitute separation based on race regardless of the benefits derived.

4. Schools, housing, spatial racism, and de facto discrimination

This Commission does not contend that there is a direct causal link between the school board's historically racially discriminatory practices and the lead in water pumped to those schools during the present water crisis. However, we include this history in our report for several important reasons.

First, school quality and racial gerrymandering of school districts certainly played a part in creating the flight of people and capital from the city. If schools within the city and the suburban fringe had been integrated from the beginning, there would have been no reason to flee to them. Housing, education and opportunity in our society are inexorably linked. Racial discrimination in any one produces discriminatory results in all.

Second, we find that many of the elements of the community schools concept implemented were premised on the inequality of races and the idea (born from decades of discriminatory practices and policies) they would coexist best if they lived separately. Race and class were considered relevant to one's capability and thus factors in what they should become and what they should be taught. Racial presumptions like these are racist, and contrary to the American ideals that should guide our government and schools. Before government (or a private foundation) seeks to supplant the will of others and make decisions for them, it must examine whether their actions lead to racially disparate outcomes. We hope that examining Flint's community schools in this context will provide a lesson for all who are given the power and responsibility to govern.

Third, we believe that the harm done to African-American children who were denied the same educational opportunities as their white counterparts, many of whom are undoubtedly still living in Flint, was irreparable. Given access to the same academic and college preparatory curricula, in the schools that were newer, more modern and less crowded, more of them would be doctors, lawyers, engineers and even elected officials today. They and their children continue to pay for our collective failure to address generations of discrimination and racial inequality.

Fourth, we believe that all discrimination shares a characteristic with a form of environmental justice we will discuss later. It has cumulative and compounding effects. The harm caused by exposure to a small amount of a pollutant from one source may not be significant by itself, but fatal if introduced along with equally 'safe' amounts of a dozen others. In this same way, the harm caused by housing discrimination will be greater on those with children who are then subjected to education discrimination. When government refuses to understand the cumulative and compounding effect of discrimination, it not only lets them down the victims, it tells them "you don't matter."

Fifth and finally, we return to the topic of *de facto* discrimination verses *de jure* discrimination and the use of *de facto* discrimination as an explanation for government actions. This Commission believes it is important to look deeper than the technical discussion about whether an action is one or the other. We believe that the differences between the two terms have less to do with what is taking place in Flint today than the too often overlooked thing they have in common. BOTH are forms of discrimination, and neither should be allowed to continue.

The discussion about whether *de facto* or *de jure* discrimination applies is about liability. It is about who is, and who is not, legally responsible for causing the harm caused by an action. Look at what the school board was saying to African Americans over and over again in the 1950s, 60s, and 70s. Strip away the legal terminology, and you get "Yes, it is racially discriminatory, but we are allowed to do it anyway."

De facto discrimination is colorblindness turned upside down. *De facto* discrimination is knowing that something will disparately harm people of color, and yet pretending to be surprised when it happens. Ignoring something is not the same as never seeing it.

De facto discrimination in Flint schools was a government entity telling a person who it is supposed to be serving, "We know your son is going to an inferior school that is falling apart and considerably overcrowded. We know that your next door neighbor's son is going to a school that is closer to your house, brand new, and at half its intended capacity. We even know that every student in the old overcrowded school is black, and every student in the new half empty school is white. But we assigned your sons to schools by address, and we didn't tell you which house to buy, so it isn't our fault."

This is the same person to who government previously said, "We financially support anyone who wants to build or buy a home in a good neighborhood. We know that our definition of a good neighborhood is one that won't let you in. We even know that if you find a good neighborhood that will let you in, it will no longer be considered to be a good neighborhood because they did. But we use exactly the same rules for everyone."

This Commission believes that one of the reasons it is so hard for government to regain the trust of Flint residents, is because we treat discrimination as though it is ACCEPTABLE when it is 'only' *de facto.*

De facto discrimination is discrimination.

De facto discrimination is not ACCEPTABLE and should NEVER be tolerated.

G. 2010-Today: The Crisis

The current Flint Water Crisis is the direct result of decisions and actions made in the last several years. From an engineering perspective it probably began in 2000 when the city's contract for water supplied by Detroit ended. Around that time decisions needed to be made about whether it was in Flint's interest to continue to source its water from Detroit, or to explore any other available options. From a liability perspective, the crisis timeline might more appropriately begin around 2010 when decisions were made that led Flint away from purchasing water from Detroit.

Neither timeline is wrong, though the 2010 timeline is particularly important. At this time, decisions were made not just about the water supply itself, but also about who the decision-makers would be, what their goals would be, and to whom they would answer. If we set back the clock to prevent the current crisis, 2010 would be far enough. Certainly, with the wisdom only hindsight provides, it would be possible to prevent this crisis by changing decisions and actions that occurred between 2010 and the Governor's emergency declaration in January 2016.

Though always cognizant of the pain and suffering endured by the people of Flint, the Commission's goal in looking back is to also determine how to prevent the NEXT crisis. The roots of the Flint Water Crisis run much deeper than decisions made in the last ten years. Preventing the 'next Flint' requires going deeper as well. We must not only examine the decisions, but also why they were necessary. We believe that the Flint Water Crisis is a symptom of a deeper disease. Simply fixing the water system, like removing a tumor, is a critical step, but it won't help the people of Flint if the cancer remains.

This Commission hopes that investigations currently underway by the Attorney General's Office identify all those individuals whose decisions and actions, whether by neglect or malfeasance, were direct causes of the lead poisoning of Flint residents, and that where appropriate these individuals are held accountable. We support these efforts and will not engage in actions that might hinder those investigations. We equally support the right of the water contamination victims to pursue legal remedies and compensation through the courts. But as important as these actions are, they are not enough.

The causes of the Flint Water Crisis are not limited to events in the present decade. Similarly, fault for the crisis cannot be laid *solely* on the decisions and actions taken during this time, or *solely* on the individuals responsible for them. Preventing the 'next Flint' will not be that easy.

We agree with the conclusion reached by the Governor's Flint Water Advisory Task Force: "The Flint Water Crisis is a story of government failure, intransigence, unpreparedness, delay, inaction and environmental injustice." And although the story of government failure the Task Force told may be accurate, we believe it is incomplete. The story they told is only the most recent chapter. We believe the

government failures that caused the Flint Water Crisis are much broader, more complex and require the additional chapters outlined in this report. If we are to prevent government's failures from causing similar crises in the future, our responses must be broader, deeper and more complex as well.

As noted earlier, fixing the problems that originated in Flint's latest chapter, will address the tumor but not the cancer. We must address the systemic problems, and must acknowledge the role that race and racism played in producing and reproducing them. Left unaddressed, this systemic racism will continue to produce racialized results.

Government, particularly state government, was slow to recognize the emergency that existed in Flint's lead-poisoned water. Evidence was ignored and facts denied. Victims were ignored, advocates demeaned. Delay in responding exacerbated the harm significantly. But in time the state did recognize there was a problem that needed to be fixed.

Government addressed the problem, by doing what it could to minimize the damage caused. People needed fresh water, and the state began to supply it. There were many challenges. Communication, language, filter installation, supply, location, transportation, delivery, and countless other issues arose. Some were predictable and could have been avoided, others not. Many were acknowledged and corrected quickly, others took more prompting, and others are still being worked on. Thus, while imperfect, the Commission finds the state's response to the crisis following the declaration of emergency, has been appropriately directed at addressing the immediate needs of Flint residents.

The governments involved (principally the state, but also local and federal), could have tried to get by doing less. But, the Commission also believes that Michiganders (including those not in Flint), would not have accepted anything less.

We cannot help but ask ourselves whether this goodwill and moral acceptance of responsibility will continue for the lifetime of all those who were harmed? Will Michigan be there for Flint's residents and their children as they continue deal with the ills resulting from the current crisis in the next 10, 20, or 40 years?

Our review of Flint's history does not suggest optimism, but the present resolve of state, local, and federal leaders does provide hope.

H. A Final Thought on the Harm Caused by Spatial Racism

Our review of Flint's history clearly establishes that past racism played an important role in creating the conditions that allowed the water contamination crisis to occur. The overtly racist practices and racialized 'neutral' policies (particularly housing policies) created the two America's described in the Kerner report, and that the Commission finds still exist in Flint today. These practices and policies lay at the heart of this water crisis.

These policies and practices fostered separation and creation of a majority black city with an outsized and decaying infrastructure and mostly white suburban communities. The mostly white suburban communities were built with a combination of wealth largely generated in the city and racially unequal distribution of government financing. People and wealth left the city supported by racialized government policies, and formed separate political entities for reasons that may not have been racist, but were certainly racialized.

The fact that civil rights laws were not violated does not mean practices implemented over the past 50 plus years did not result in *de facto* discrimination and disparate impact.

Race, racialization, racism (particularly spatial), and *de facto* discrimination are the heart and soul of this crisis.

What does this mean for the white people who live in Flint who are victims of this water crisis every much as their black neighbors? Why should the skin color of someone who works or spent time in Flint and consumed the poisoned water matter?

Simply stated, they too are victims of racism by association.

White families who stayed behind while other fled, lost the value of their real estate investments the same way the black families moving in did. Their lost retirement nest egg, or lost inheritance is not less harmful to them than it is to the African Americans who had no choice of living elsewhere.

> "White victims of racist acts and policies based on malice or disregard for blacks are victims of racism."

White victims of racist acts and policies based on malice or disregard for blacks are victims of racism.

And whether the victim is black or white, racism isn't fixed by not repeating it; it is like a plague that engulfs everyone in its path.

III. ENVIRONMENTAL INJUSTICE, ROLE OF STRUCTURAL RACIALIZATION IN FLINT'S WATER

NOTHING ABOUT US WITHOUT US

A. Environmental justice

Environmental justice is a comparatively new concept. It followed in the footsteps of the civil rights movement, and represented a coming together with a growing environmental movement. It began in the early 1980s as various community leaders recognized that low income and communities of color were subjected to greater amounts of pollution and suffered greater adverse health effects than did others. The movement first attained national attention in 1982 when the NAACP and a local community in North Carolina joined in protest over dumping soil contaminated with polychlorinated biphenyls (PCBs) in a landfill near a poor, predominantly minority community.[223]

The movement gained steam when the United Church of Christ and the Government Accounting Office (GAO) conducted two separate studies in 1983 and 1987, showing that hazardous waste facilities were disproportionally located near communities with largely black and brown populations. The Environmental Protection Agency created its Office of Environmental Justice in 1992, and in 1994, the National Institutes of Health and the Center for Disease Control joined with other government agencies, researchers, health care professionals and community residents to host a "Symposium on Health Research and Needs to Ensure Environmental Justice." Following the symposium, and also in 1994, President Clinton signed an executive order adopting its goals as government policy.[224]

---

[223] Advancing Environmental Justice, National Institute of Environmental Health Sciences (July 2015), 5, available at < https://www.niehs.nih.gov/research/supported/assets/docs/a_c/advancing_environmental_justice_508.pdf> (accessed February 12, 2017).
[224] *Id.* at 5-7.

According to the written testimony of University of Michigan Professor Paul Mohai,[225] numerous studies have demonstrated that the racial composition of communities is a statistically significant predictor of where environmental burdens are concentrated.[226] Specifically, Professor Mohai cites the 1987 United Church of Christ study, *Toxic Wastes and Race in the United States,*[227] which found that "among multiple variables examined, race was the best predictor of which areas in the U.S. contain hazardous waste facilities and which do not, even when controlling for income, property values, and the amount of hazardous wastes generated." The results have been consistently replicated.[228] Improved data collection including Geographic information Systems (GIS) data have shown the link between racial and socioeconomic disparities and the location of environmental burdens to be even greater than fist believed thought.[229] Even when socioeconomic disparities and other 'colorblind' variables

---

[225] Professor Paul Mohai is a Professor in the School of Natural Resources at the University of Michigan. Professor Mohai's teaching and research interests are focused on environmental justice, public opinion and the environment, and influences on environmental policy making. He is a founder of the Environmental Justice Program at the University of Michigan and a major contributor to the growing body of quantitative research examining disproportionate environmental burdens and their impacts on low income and people of color communities.

[226] Professor Mohai's written testimony is available at < http://www.michigan.gov/documents/mdcr/Mohai_Testimony_-_MCRC_-_Oct_1_2016_536288_7.pdf> (accessed February 12, 2017), hereinafter referred to as Mohai Testimony.

[227] Commission for Racial Justice, United Church of Christ, *Toxic Waste in the United States: A National Report on the Racial and Socio-Economic Characteristics of Communities with Hazardous Waste Sites*, available at <https://www.nrc.gov/docs/ML1310/ML13109A339.pdf> (accessed February 12, 2017).

[228] Mohai Testimony at 4, citing Mohai, P., and B. Bryant. 1992. "Environmental Racism: Reviewing the Evidence." Pages 163-176 in B. Bryant and P. Mohai, eds., *Race and the Incidence of Environmental Hazards: A Time for Discourse* (Boulder, CO: Westview Press); Goldman, B. A. (1994). *Not just prosperity: Achieving sustainability with environmental justice.* Washington DC: National Wildlife Federation; and Ringquist, EJ. 2005. Assessing evidence of environmental inequities: a meta-analysis. *J. Policy Anal. Manag.* 24:223–47.

[229] *Id.,* citing Bullard, Robert D., Paul Mohai, Robin Saha, Beverly Wright. 2007. *Toxic Wastes and Race at Twenty 1987–2007: Grassroots Struggles to Dismantle Environmental Racism in the United States.* Cleveland, OH: United Church Christ Justice Witness Ministery; Chakraborty J, Maantay J A and Brender J D. 2011. "Disproportionate proximity to environmental health hazards: methods, models, and measurement." *Am. J. Public Health* 101: S27–3; Collins, Mary B., Iaan Munoz and Joseph JaJa 2016. "Linking 'toxic outliers' to environmental justice communities." *Environmental Research Letters* 11 015004; Mohai, Paul, and Robin Saha. 2006. "Reassessing Racial and Socioeconomic Disparities in Environmental Justice Research." *Demography* 43(2): 383-399; Mohai, Paul, and Robin Saha. 2007. "Racial Inequality in the Distribution of Hazardous Waste: A National-Level Reassessment."

are accounted for, race and the location of environmental hazards statistically remain closely tied.[230]

Professor Mohai also provided many in-depth case studies of specific environmental justice controversies in cities across much of the United States.[231] Here too studies consistently reveal the residents of impacted communities to predominantly be poor people of color.

Many researchers believe that communities of color are targeted for hazardous waste sites, polluting industrial facilities, and other locally unwanted land uses (LULUs) because they lack the resources and political clout to fend off the siting of such facilities. They are often seen as the "paths of least resistance" by industry and government.[232] At the same time, when their communities are found to be contaminated with unacceptable levels of pollution and toxins, low priority is given to addressing their concerns.[233]

The most common definition of environmental justice (EJ) is "all people and communities are entitled to equal protection of environmental and public health laws and regulations."[234] Simply put, the concept of environmental justice provides that everybody has an equal right to live in a clean, healthy and safe environment, and when it comes to decisions that involve or affect their environment, everybody should have an equal voice. However, this statement presents two questions: What is 'environmental'? And an equal voice in what arena?

Social Problems 54(3): 343-370; Mohai, Paul, and Robin Saha. 2015(b). "Which came first, people or pollution? Assessing the disparate siting and post-siting demographic change hypotheses of environmental injustice." *Environ. Res. Lett.* 10 115008: 1-17.

[230]Ash and Fetter (2005); Bullard et al. (2007); Mohai et al. (2009); Pais et al (2014); Zwickl et al. (2014)

[231] Bullard (2000); Bullard and Wright (2012); Cole and Foster (2001); Kemberling and Roberts (2009); Lee (1992); Lerner (2012). See also the Environmental Justice Organization, Liability, and Trade (EJOLT) Atlas of Environmental Justice Conflicts (https://ejatlas.org/country/united-states-of-america), which identifies the "40 Most Influential Environmental Justice Conflicts in U.S. History" as determined from a survey of environmental justice leaders in the U.S. (Grafton et al. 2015).

[232] Bullard and Wright (2012); Mohai and Saha (2015); Pastor, Sadd, and Hipp (2001); Taylor (2014)

[233] Bryant and Mohai (1992); Bullard and Wright (2012); Lerner (2012)

[234] Mohai, written testimony at 4.

When we think of environmental issues, water pipes, water filtration and aging infrastructure, and government decisions related to them, do not immediately come to mind. Public policy issues that are considered to be environmental are typically related to preserving the environment itself. What affect do auto emissions have on greenhouse gasses or the ozone layer? How can we preserve forests and marshlands?

However, one cannot consider water filtration without considering the water source and the pollution that must be filtered out to make the water consumable. Water quality itself is an environmental issue, but does it stop being one at the moment when the water is piped from the source, or perhaps at some specific point during the filtration process?

The Michigan Civil Rights Commission agrees with the Governor's 2016 Flint Water Crisis Task Force (Task Force)[235] that the delivery of contaminated water to the people of Flint is an environmental justice issue. It includes the decision to use the Flint River as a water source in spite of the pollutants it contains and the subsequent decision not to treat the water with anticorrosion chemicals. The right to clean, healthy, safe water is certainly a right that every individual is entitled to depend. In the case of Flint, the constructs of environmental justice are both relevant and helpful to understanding the injustice represented by Flint's water contamination.

The question of the arena in which each of us is entitled to an equal voice is necessary to any discussion of democracy and civil rights. It is particularly relevant to the Flint Water Crisis. Raw majority rule can be manipulated by adjusting the size those included in a decision, civil rights cannot. Civil (and human) rights require recognizing fundamental rights that everyone holds equally and cannot be stripped from a minority based only on the will of a majority.

If a decision to place a toxic waste disposal site is left only to adjacent property owners, no site would ever be built. It may be equally impossible to place a site within any given city if it requires a majority vote of only residents of that city. Thus, when it is determined that such a site is necessary for the 'common good,' such placement decisions are often made at a county, state or even federal level. While enlarging the arena in which the decision is made to all those who may benefit from the 'common good' may be necessary, environmental justice examines the relationship between those who share the common benefit and those who bear the localized harm.

B. Environmental Justice Principles:

The Final Report of the Governor's Task Force divided the issue of environmental justice into "two fundamental principles: (1) the fair, non-discriminatory treatment of all people; and (2) the provision for meaningful public involvement of all people regardless of race, color, national

---

[235] see fn 4.

origin or income – in government decision-making regarding environmental laws, regulations and policies."[236] These two principles are essentially the same as those the U.S. Environmental Protection Agency (EPA) calls "fair treatment" and "meaningful involvement."[237]

Dr. Paul Mohai urged this Commission to recognize the "17 Principles of Environmental Justice."[238] These were the product of the 1991 "First National People of Color Environmental Leadership Summit" and have been adopted or used by many examining environmental justice issues since. This Commission recognizes the importance of the Leadership Summit's early work in this area, and values their 17-pronged approach, but we cannot formally adopt it as several of their concerns (*e.g.,* international law) are beyond the scope of this Commission's authority and scope.

---

[236] Final Report of the Governor's Flint Water Advisory Task Force at p. 54.

[237] The EPA more specifically defines fair treatment as the principle that "no group of people should bear a disproportionate share of the negative environmental consequences resulting from industrial, governmental and commercial operations or policies." The EPA's definition of meaningful involvement requires that "a) People have an opportunity to participate in decisions about activities that may affect their environment and/or health, b) The public's contribution can influence the regulatory agency's decision, c) Community concerns will be considered in the decision making process, and d) Decision makers will seek out and facilitate the involvement of those potentially affected." <https://www.epa.gov/environmentaljustice/learn-about-environmental-justice> (accessed February 15, 2017).

[238] Available at < http://www.ejnet.org/ej/principles.html > (accessed February 15, 2017).

Dr. Mohai also urges recognition of a three-part approach originally set forth by Professor Robert Kuehn,[239] a recognized expert in the field. Kuehn's "Taxonomy of Environmental Justice" breaks environmental justice down into three principles: distributive justice, procedural justice, and corrective justice. The first two principles are essentially the same as the two already discussed. However, the addition of the third concern "corrective justice" is significant. Dr. Mohai explains that Professor Kuehn describes corrective justice as both punitive and restorative. "Corrective justice involves not only the just administration of punishment to those who break the law, but also a duty to repair the losses for which one is responsible." It involves both "fairness in the way punishments for law breaking are assigned" and in the way that the "damages inflicted on individuals and communities are addressed."

The Commission believes it is essential to include the principle of corrective justice in any environmental justice analysis. Citizens are protected from future injustices when decision makers know there are consequences for committing them. Public trust in the system may not be necessarily be restored by penalizing violations of the law, but not punishing government actors or punishing only those responsible for following decisions without including those who made them, further erodes the public's confidence in government. Public confidence is dependent on government taking action to repair and recompense any harms that may result from its policies, especially when such harms are suffered only by an identifiable subgroup of the total population.

We believe that the only way environmental justice can be achieved, and the only way government can show that environmental injustices are unacceptable, is for government to accept responsibility when they occur, punish any wrongdoers, and address the harm caused. Flint residents repeatedly testified that government could not be trusted and did not have their best interests in mind. Taking responsibility by adopting the two-pronged approach found in the Task Force Report as well as assessing Professor Kuehn's three principles (distributive justice, procedural justice, and corrective justice) are critical steps to not only repair and recompense harm, but to rebuild trust.

---

[239] Currently an associate dean at the Washington University School of Law, Professor Kuehn focuses his teaching on environmental law, clinical legal education and professional responsibility and has published extensively on such topics as environmental justice, environmental enforcement, environmental science and natural resources conservation. He previously was with the U.S. Department of Justice where he brought enforcement actions on behalf of the U.S. EPA.

C. Environmental Racism

In his testimony, Dr. Mohai referenced the definition of environmental racism offered by Professor Robert D. Bullard,[240] who Mohai described as "perhaps the most prolific writer and best known and influential national and international leader on the issue of environment justice." Environmental justice is "any policy, practice, or directive that differentially affects or disadvantages (whether intended or unintended) individuals, groups, or communities base on race or color."[241]

As the Governor's Task Force noted, "Environmental injustice is not about malevolent intent or deliberate attacks on specific populations, nor does it come in measures that overtly violate civil rights." This raises the question of whether or not the actions surrounding the Flint Water Crisis raises to the level of environmental racism. Bullard has stated that environmental racism includes the deliberate targeting of communities of color or the systematic exclusion of people of color from leadership roles in decisions regarding the production of environmental conditions that affect their lives and livelihoods. Focusing solely on "motive or intent" may be too limiting a factor in distinguishing between environmental injustice and environmental racism. Instead, the Commission believes that finding environmental racism does not require that government's motives be racial, or that government actors be racists. Environmental racism occurs when people of color repeatedly suffer disproportionate risks and harms from policies and decisions that equally benefit all. This injustice is even greater when the benefits of those policies and decisions harm people of color while disproportionately benefiting others.

D. Distributive Justice

---

[240] Robert D. Bullard is often described as the father of environmental justice. He is the author of eighteen books that address sustainable development, environmental racism, urban land use, and many similar topics. See <http://drrobertbullard.com/biography/> (accessed February 15, 2017).

[241] Robert Bullard, Environment and Morality: Confronting Environmental Racism in the United States, United States Research Institute for Social Development, October 2004. Available at http://www.unrisd.org/80256B3C005BCCF9/httpNetITFramePDF?ReadForm&parentunid=543B2B250E647452802 56B6D005788F7&parentdoctype=paper&netitpath=80256B3C005BCCF9/(httpAuxPages)/543B2B250E6474528025 6B6D005788F7/$file/bullard.pdf> (accessed February 15, 2017).

The EPA defines fair treatment as the principle that "no group of people should bear a disproportionate share of the negative environmental consequences resulting from industrial, governmental and commercial operations or policies."[242] However, in spite of the EPA's declaration that no group shall bear a disproportionate burden, it has been long and well established that America's poor, urban, and particularly communities of color do bear a "disproportionate share of the negative consequences" that result from environmental decisions.

For example, Professor Michael Mascarenhas,[243] in his oral and written testimony to this Commission cites a 1983 study conducted by the U.S. General Accounting Office (GAO) that examined four licensed commercial hazardous waste facilities in three southern states. Using 1980 census data, the GAO compared the census tracks for ZIP codes within four miles of each facility, and compared them with ZIP codes that had no hazardous waste treatment, storage, or disposal facilities. The study found that three of the four sites were located in predominantly black communities and that in all four sites the black population in the surrounding census areas had a lower mean income than the mean income for all races combined, and they represented the majority of those below the poverty level.[244]

Also cited before this Commission, was the 1987 study by the United Church of Christ Commission on Racial Justice entitled *Toxic Wastes and Race in the United States*.[245] This was the first national study to use the same "unit-hazard coincidence" method (ZIP codes and census data) as the GAO study. This study found that race was the most significant factor in determining where waste facilities were located in the United States.

Specifically, the *Toxic Wastes and Race* study found that ZIP codes with no hazardous waste treatment, storage, or disposal facilities had 12.3% minority population, ZIP codes with one such facility had about double that figure, and in ZIP codes with more than one facility (as well

---

[242] *See* <https://www.epa.gov/environmentaljustice/learn-about-environmental-justice> (accessed February 15, 2017).

[243] Associate Professor, Rensselaer Polytechnic Institute, Science and Technology Studies Department. He is currently working on a project on the intersecting pathways of citizen science, civic engagement, emergency management, and environmental justice in the Flint Water Crisis. <http://www.sts.rpi.edu/pl/faculty/michael-mascarenhas> (accessed February 15, 2017).

[244] Mascarenhas written testimony at p. 6.

[245] *See* fn 223.

as those with each of the five largest landfills in the U.S.), the percentage of minorities jumped to 37.6%. This study also discovered that three out of five African Americans and Hispanic Americans lived in communities with one or more uncontrolled toxic waste sites, and that half of Asian/Pacific Islander Americans and Native Americans lived in such communities.

The *Toxic Wastes and Race* report concluded that race was the *primary* predictor of where hazardous wastes would be located in the United States. The relationship of race and hazardous waste was determined to be more direct than, for example, household income or home values.

Most significant, in 1992 the EPA published a report entitled *Environmental Equity: Reducing Risks for All Communities*.[246] The EPA specifically found that "Racial minority and low-income populations experience higher than average exposures to selected air pollutants, [and] hazardous waste facilities."[247] This report was the first official recognition by the federal government that minority and low-income populations in the U.S. are disproportionately exposed to environmental hazards. The EPA further recognized that while such "(e)xposure does not always result in an immediate or acute health effect, high exposures, and the possibility of chronic effects, are nevertheless a clear cause for health concerns."

Another factor in distributive justice or fair treatment is the relationship between benefit and cost. Environmental decisions are made by weighing whether the public good created justifies the potential public harm caused. Environmental justice not only asks whether the harms are evenly borne by all, it also examines the relationship between communities that benefit and those that pay the price. Distributive injustice is greatest when the benefits are unevenly shared, i.e., the people who receive the greatest benefit are those that are least exposed to the consequences.

Thus, the Commission is confronted with two inescapable and irreconcilable facts: (1) Environmental justice requires that no group bear more of the harm caused by environmental decisions than do other groups, and (2) People of color are disproportionately harmed by those decisions. By definition, this is environmental injustice and environmental racism.

1. Distributive justice, individual self-interest, racialization, and systemic racism

---

[246] The full report consists of two volumes. Volume One is the *Workgroup Report to the Administrator,* available at <https://books.google.com/books?id=synkxbLVyjQC&pg=PP1&source=gbs_selected_pages&cad=2#v=onepage&q&f=false> (accessed February 15, 2017) and Volume Two is entitled *Supporting Document,* available at < https://books.google.com/books?id=synkxbLVyjQC&pg=PP1&source=gbs_selected_pages&cad=2#v=onepage&q&f=false> (accessed February 15, 2017).

[247] It also found a higher exposure to contaminated fish and agricultural pesticides in the workplace.

As we saw when we examined housing and the history of white flight, our political and economic system can cause good people with good motives to not recognize that their decisions have racialized outcomes. A family that knows they have a limited time opportunity to trade a house decreasing in value for one currently at the same price but increasing in value are not racists if they decide to move. It may well be racism that is driving the property value down, but even a family that would prefer to live in a diverse neighborhood must weigh that desire against the financial (and if they have children, the educational) costs of staying.

Whether structural, or systemic, racialized outcomes have a similar impact on distributive environmental justice. The owner of a manufacturing business wishing to build a new plant will most likely look for inexpensive land already zoned for manufacturing. That owner will not purposefully buy land upwind from residences inhabited primarily by people of color, but (s)he will almost likely end up purchasing exactly that.

The construction of industrial polluters almost exclusively near communities of color is a racialized outcome, yet the decisions to build in these areas are likely driven by economics, not race. Good people, making good business decisions, may never even consider race as part of their decision making process, and yet make decisions that produce and perpetuate racialized outcomes, and are the result of a complex and interconnected socio-political system.

Some may make a chicken/egg type argument that environmental risks don't always move to lower priced land located in areas made up of people of color; sometimes people move into areas where the risks are already present because they can find affordable housing. The Commission finds the matter of which pattern dominates to be an interesting academic question, for those who work in the environmental justice field. However, we observe that there is unquestionably a considerable amount of each. More important, whether toxic waste and industrial polluters move to impoverished areas seeking low cost land, or their presence causes residents who can afford it to vacate the surrounding properties by selling to others with less resources, the system is structured in a way that ensures the ultimate losers will be those with the least resources – that is, persons of color.

Political factors can also work very much like economic factors to 'steer' industry to areas that are majority people of color. By political factors we are not suggesting that the business owners are partisan, only that they understand the political hurdles they face if they need any zoning, regulatory, or similar approval to operate. The owner of any business that will require such approvals has a great incentive to locate wherever opposition is likely to be the least, or the least effective.

Businesses scouting locations to build toxic waste facilities may never (consciously at least) consider race at all. They are more likely to be looking for locations where people who might oppose the industry are the least likely to be politically effective, than they are to care about why. Where are community members likely to have multiple jobs or household responsibilities that could prevent them from having the time to personally participate in a political process?

Where do people have the least resources to put up a fight in opposition? Or perhaps they will ask themselves where the community members most likely to lack the education, skills, or confidence (either in themselves or the process) to permit them to effectively leverage the political process? While each of these questions might be a legitimate business concern, and while not one of them is directly racial, their answers will nonetheless direct the business to communities of color.

Industrial accidents affecting a neighborhood likewise have a disparate racial impact. By definition we don't know where our environment will next be damaged by an "accident." Still, we can state without equivocation that, if the accident is in a permanent facility and is not so massive as to cover a very large geographical area, it will disparately harm people of color because they are who lives nearby. Yes, it will also negatively and disparately harm low income families and therefore constitutes distributive and environmental injustice. Spatial segregation now becomes the form that is leveraged to ensure that environmental risks will not threaten affluent communities while disproportionally harming communities of color.

> "When benefits are shared equally, but the harms and risks are repeatedly distributed so as to impact only a few, it is an environmental injustice…"

When benefits are shared equally, but the harms and risks are repeatedly distributed so as to impact only a few, it is an environmental injustice and may, in some cases, even rise to the level of environmental racism.

2. Distributive justice, structural racialization, and cumulative impact

Cumulative impact is a simple concept. It is intuitive, obvious, and in some cases scientifically provable. It can also be difficult to establish and impossible to quantify. That we have collectively allowed our inability or unwillingness to quantify the cumulative impacts of environmental hazards and harms to prevent us from properly addressing them is possibly the most difficult aspect of environmental justice, and likely the most harmful.

At its core, cumulative impact is simply the idea that in scientific study and in regulatory requirements we assess things in isolation, but in the real world we experience them in unison. We determine the level at which a chemical in our air, water or food becomes harmful, and we treat anything less as safe – and we do so as though our lives mirror test conditions.

It is as though we believed that, because we determined someone could safely lift a 100-pound boulder, we believe they can "safely" carry four 25 pound boulders. Would we require a soldier wearing 20 pounds of armor to carry a 5-pound weapon, 20 pounds of ammunition, 5 pounds of rations, 5 pounds of water, 10 pounds of night and weather gear, a radio and spare batteries, a flash light, and miscellaneous other gear on a 20-mile hike, all based on a determination that it was safe to carry 50 pounds on a three mile hike? Maybe so, but not without the soldiers paying a price.[248]

Why then do we even consider permitting a company to construct a second facility adjacent to one that already exists without first assessing and considering the cumulative impact of the two in combination?   It would be more appropriate to determine where the existing air quality was less polluted, and (if we still thought the common good made it necessary at all) locate the new source of 'safe' amounts of pollution at that location.

Cumulative impact in this respect requires government not just to assess emissions at their origin (*e.g.*, at the top of a smokestack), but also at its destination (*e.g.*, a residence) and that the assessment examines it in combination with other emissions.

When people breathe air, they inhale everything in it. Yet we routinely cluster sources of pollution and other environmental harms in one place while making little effort to consider the cumulative impact of doing so.

We know that chemicals in pollutants (and sometimes even 'non-harmful' irritants like non-toxic smoke) often have a greater negative impact on some people than others. For example, they are likely to aggravate and worsen a person's asthma, and more likely to adversely impact someone with an immune deficiency. We also know that infants and senior citizens are more likely than others to suffer negative consequence from the same exposure.

If we know that something will cause greater harm to people with 'preexisting conditions,' should we seek to avoid locating it where the greatest concentration of people with those conditions reside? Distributive environmental justice requires that we should at least take this into consideration.

The Commission understands that measuring or predicting specific cumulative effects is difficult, if not impossible. The Commission does not suggest that cumulative effect can always be quantified, or that it is an exact science. However, the Commission asserts that some cumulative impacts, even if unquantifiable, are sufficiently demonstrable and/or so widely accepted, that the failure to consider them should be considered environmental injustice.

For example, the Commission believes it is distributive environmental injustice when government:

- Fails to consider high childhood asthma rates in a downwind community when assessing a request to begin or increase a potentially harmful emission.
- Fails to consider the current air quality of an area when assessing a request to begin or increase an emission.

---

[248] See, for example, http://www.seattletimes.com/nation-world/weight-of-war-gear-that-protects-troops-also-injures-them/

- Fails to consider other environmental harms and risks like water quality when assessing a request to begin or increase an air emission.
- Fails to consider existing aggravating factors like poor health, lack of health care, and malnutrition, and/or lack of access to healthy foods.

The Commission stresses that the failure to consider cumulative effects in examples like those above is unjust. By allowing environmental harm and risks to exist or be placed in locations where they will do the most harm, instead of where they will do the least, is a good example of just how insidious systemic racism can be. This serves to propagate environmental injustice disproportionately effecting African Americans and/or other people of color when decisions are being made.

3. Distributive justice, cumulative impact, and the ongoing recovery in Flint:

There is one more aspect related to cumulative impact and distributive environmental justice that is especially relevant to the Flint Water Crisis, and that continues to be a problem in Flint. We have noted that the failure to consider health when assessing a request to begin or increase an emission can result in maximizing rather than minimizing the harm suffered by some to secure a benefit for all. A similar harm can be caused by a failure to take existing health conditions into account when responding to an existing environmental hazard.

A good example of properly addressing this concern in Flint is state and local government efforts to ensure that proper nutrition is provided to the city's children exposed to lead. This is necessary to permit their bodies to best absorb lead and counter its effects, thereby minimizing the damage the lead already ingested will cause. Such efforts might be unnecessary if the same crisis had occurred elsewhere, but the cumulative effect of lead consumption and malnutrition requires that it be done here. Similarly, we should not ignore the cumulative harm to the children of Flint by the trauma of dealing with the daily challenges brought by the contamination of their drinking water, and by the trauma of exposure to media and other public discussion about how this will affect their future and speculating on their potentially bleak prospects.

In reviewing cumulative affect the Commission questions whether governments at all levels have fully considered how residents may be affected on a long-term basis due to a compromised immune system or other health problems due to the contamination of the drinking water. For example, can we definitively say that otherwise safe levels of a substance cannot cause skin rashes to persons exposed to lead, or do we just not have evidence they do?

In summary, we do not want to neglect the role of cumulative effect that can be caused by the multiple afflictions often experienced by people in communities like Flint. Considering them only separately not only fails to recognize the actual harm being caused, it contributes to a lack of trust in government, and what government says.

E. Procedural Justice

The EPA's definition of the meaningful involvement inherent to procedural justice requires that: "a) People have an opportunity to participate in decisions about activities that may affect their environment and/or health, b) The public's contribution can influence the regulatory agency's decision, c) Community concerns will be considered in the decision making process, and d) Decision makers will seek out and facilitate the involvement of those potentially affected."[249]

1. Procedural Justice and Emergency Management

While Michigan's emergency manager Law will be separately addressed elsewhere report, it is recognized here because, at least as it operated with respect to the switch of Flint's water source, the law functionally denied any semblance of the meaningful involvement required to meet the definition of procedural justice.

In his testimony, Dr. Mohai called the emergency manager law "possibly the single most important violation of the principle of procedural justice in the case of the Flint Water Crisis."[250] Although we decline to rank procedural justice violations, we agree that the absence of public input either directly or through officials they elected, is a very significant violation of the principles of environmental justice. It is made even more substantial because nobody was accountable, or even responsive, to the people who voiced concerns after the water source had been switched.

However, neither the Emergency Manager Law, nor the question of who made the decision to switch Flint's water source, tells the whole story of the procedural injustices inflicted on the people of Flint.

2. Procedural Justice and Michigan's Environmental Justice Plans

An equally strong case can be made that, even with the emergency manager law, and even with an emergency manager in place in Flint, this crisis may have been averted, or mitigated, if the state had adopted and implemented either of two proposed Environmental Justice Plans. We will never know.

As Professor Sara R. Gosman[251] stated it in her testimony: "The story of Flint is not just one of government indifference about the health of a poor community of color, it is also the story of a

---

[249] <https://www.epa.gov/environmentaljustice/learn-about-environmental-justice> (accessed February 15, 2017).
[250] Hearing 3, Session 1, at 25:05.
[251] An Assistant Professor at the University of Arkansas, School of Law, Ms. Gosman was a lecturer at the University of Michigan Law School and a member of the Governor's Environmental Justice Working Group from 2008-10.

broken environmental policy making process, in which economic interests played an outsized role and environmental justice is viewed as a special interest issue, rather than an issue of civil rights."[252]

Neither environmental justice, nor the procedural justice requirement to provide the public with meaningful participation in decisions that affect their health, are new concerns in Michigan. Professor Gosman testified that the DEQ's first environmental justice working group issued a report in 1999 identifying four key issues: (1) the role of local government, (2) identification of environmental justice areas, (3) public participation, and (4) the definition of disparate impacts.[253] The group was, however, unable to come up with a complete plan, and the recommendations it made were not implemented.

In 2003, then DEQ Director Steven Chester tasked an Agency Environmental Advisory Council with making recommendations on how the interests of environmental justice could be pursued. The recommendations presented to Governor Jennifer Granholm in 2006, included forming an interagency working group to be advised by a citizens' panel and requiring individual agencies to adopt their own environmental justice plans. More noteworthy was a recommendation that the Governor consider "mechanisms for individual communities to further environmental justice interests," including a *petition process* to address the concerns that any group identifiable by race, color, national origin, or income, is or will be disproportionately and negatively impacted as a result of the development, implementation, and enforcement of environmental laws."[254]

These recommendations led Governor Granholm to issue Executive Directive 2007-23. The Executive Directive instructed DEQ to develop and implement an environmental justice plan that included requirements to "[i]dentify and address discriminatory public health or environmental effects of state laws, regulations, policies, and activities," and to "provide policies and procedures for state departments and agencies to ensure that environmental justice principals [sic] are incorporated into departmental and agency decision-making and practices."[255] Again, the most striking item in the 2007 directive was the requirement to "recommend *mechanisms for members of the public*, communities, and groups to assert adverse or disproportionate social, economic or environmental impact upon a community and request responsive state action."

A workgroup that included 26 individuals from state and local governments, industry, environmental organizations, American Indian tribes, and academia was convened in 2008.

---

[252] Hearing 3, Session 2, at 17:25.
[253] Gosman, written testimony p. 4.
[254] *Id.* at p. 5 (emphasis added).
[255] *Id.*, citing 35 Mich. Exec. Directive No. 2007-23 (2007).

This group was divided into six subcommittees, with each assigned to tackle a key issue and bring their proposed solution back to the group as a whole. Among the key issues to be considered were disparate impacts, providing for public participation, and development of a petition process.

Both the subcommittees and the workgroup as a whole worked primarily by what Professor Kyle Powys Whyte described as a "consensus" process. That is, when differing interests had differing opinions, a matter was talked through to find common ground rather than by majority rule.[256]

a.   The Rejected 2009 Environmental Justice Plan

The workgroup's efforts resulted in its adoption of a proposed Michigan Environmental Justice Plan in 2009 (the 2009 Plan). This plan was developed over the preceding ten years. Former DEQ Director, Steve Chester, indicated that several representatives from business organizations on the workgroup agreed to release the 2009 draft plan for public comment but did NOT agree with all of the draft plan's recommendations. Pursuant to the Governor's Directive, the plan, when published for public comment, included a section on cumulative impact as part of the effort to "[i]dentify and address discriminatory public health or environmental effects of state laws, regulations, policies, and activities." It provided for integration of environmental justice principles into the work of all government agencies, and more specifically, for training of state employees on the principles of environmental justice to ensure that they become "incorporated into departmental and agency decision-making and practices."

The 2009 Plan created a petition process and interagency response that addressed the Governor's mandate to provide "mechanisms for members of the public, communities, and groups to assert adverse or disproportionate social, economic or environmental impact upon a community and request responsive state action." The plan would have permitted residents of a community like Flint to ask the interagency workgroup to look at an environmental justice concern from the differing perspectives of multiple agencies not directly involved in the decision-making. Instead of Flint citizens having their environmental concerns addressed only by DEQ, they would have been able to raise the concerns with a group that included agencies looking at the implications on matters such as public health, education, and civil rights.

Professor Gosman describes the petition process in greater detail:

> "[C]ommunities could file a petition with an Interdepartmental Working Group (IWG) composed of representatives from the Governor's office, the DEQ, the then-Department of Community Health, the DCR, and other state agencies. The petition would require the signatures of 50 residents, including at least 25 from the affected community. In determining whether to accept a petition, the IWG

---

[256] Associate Professor, Michigan State University.

would consider whether there was a likely disparate impact; the severity of the environmental, economic and/or social impact; the severity of the other environmental, economic, and/or social issues facing the community and cumulative effects; the authority of the state to address the problem; the ability of coordinated state action to resolve the problem successfully; whether there was a pending lawsuit or administrative challenge; and other concerns raised by the community. If the IWG accepted the petition, a state environmental justice coordinator in the Governor's office would work with coordinators in the DEQ and other agencies to develop an action plan."[257]

It is important to note that, contrary to later industry protestations, the proposed language of the 2009 Plan explicitly provided that the petition process "is not intended to interfere with existing permitting or project timelines," that "denial of a petition is not subject to appeal," and that "commitments are based on the agencies' existing legal authority and are conducted within the agencies' existing legal duties."[258]

As previously stated, once the plan was published for public comment, industry representatives raised objections. Four of the six industry representatives who offered testimony in opposition to the plan during the public comment period had been members of the workgroup.[259]

It is clear that the petition process was intended to protect the public's right to meaningful participation. If DEQ did not on its own pay serious attention to the people of Flint, perhaps requiring them to share and discuss their testing data with representatives from the Department of Health and Human Services in the presence of people from the Governor's office would have elevated the attention level.

This Commission agrees with Professor Gosman who in her written testimony states:

> If the Draft Environmental Justice Plan had been adopted and implemented, I cannot say for sure that the Flint water crisis would have been prevented. But it would have made it much less likely. The petition process in the draft plan was designed for situations such as the one in Flint. The process would have allowed Flint residents to elevate their concerns by filing a petition with the IWG. Because the IWG would have included directors of the DEQ and the Department of Health and Human Services as well as the Governor's environmental policy advisor, there would have been recognition at the highest levels of the problems

---

[257] Gosman written testimony at p. 6-7.
[258] Gosman written testimony at p. 7.
[259] Gosman written testimony at p. 8.

in Flint. And if the IWG accepted the petition, there would have been an action plan to address the problems.

It is all but certain that the petition process would at least have resulted in a more careful review of decisions to permanently switch from the Detroit water system to the KWA system and to use the Flint River as a temporary water source. It is possible that such decisions could have been different after such a review. Even if they had not been, the involvement of other agencies could have resulted in greater and more timely attention to details like whether treating the Flint River water to control bacterial concerns would result in it becoming corrosive and whether there was also a treatment available for the resulting corrosiveness. Particularly after GM indicated the water was corroding parts and machinery, it is difficult to imagine that an interagency group would not have quickly questioned whether the water corroding automobile parts might also be corroding the water pipes.

Most certain to have changed the outcome of the Flint Water Crisis would have been the petition process allowing Flint residents to voice their concerns about the quality of the water, its smell, color, and taste, and the rashes it caused. The petition process would have required that data was shared and reviewed by an interagency group.

If the results that some DEQ employees found alarming were shared with health officials, and if those health officials were accountable as part of the decision-making process, what else might have been done differently? If, at an interagency meeting like the one contemplated by the 2009 Plan, someone simply asking the question of what might be different if Flint were a wealthy community made up of politically connected white people, could very well have prevented or at least lessened the harms caused to the people government should have been protecting.

The Commission notes that the petition process and the need to consider cumulative effect were eliminated from the 2009 Plan and if adopted could have made a difference. However, we will never know for certain. What we do know is that 2009 Plan, after the departure of Steve Chester, was substantially changed and redrafted leading to the creation of the 2010 Environmental Justice Plan.

b.   The Disregarded 2010 Environmental Justice Plan

Professor Gosman testified that "The Flint water crisis to me is a textbook example of environmental injustice. Members of the Flint community were not fairly treated, nor given the opportunity for meaningful participation in the decisions that affected their health. The environmental justice plan that could have given the community a voice was first weakened, then never implemented."[260]

In his testimony, Professor Mascarenhas noted, "Equality of persons, which is at the center of environmental theories of justice, starts with an assumption of equal respect for all citizens."[261] Yet, experts recognize that environmental injustice often results, at least in part, from a lack of respect by those who make decisions for those who are affected by the decisions.

As Professor Whyte described it: "Oftentimes when community members and residents feel there is something wrong with the environment and they are being affected disproportionately, they are not recognized in their own experiences and their problems are not dealt with quickly – and they are oftentimes insulted, disrespected and not listened to."[262]

Professor Mohai similarly stated that "[t]he almost utter lack of concern when the populations get impacted and people's health are damaged – And I have to say that in the case of Flint, where the government response was, not only was slow, but the first step wasn't to try to solve the problem, it was to try and discount the residents' complaints, belittle them, and even when the first outside scientific evidence came in, for example from Dr. Marc Edwards, there was even an attempt to discredit that."[263]

What if the government officials and employees who dealt with the initial complaints about the Flint water had received training in procedural justice and understood that the history of environmental injustices included a common element of ignoring those actually being affected? Properly trained government employees could have understood environmental justice principles, such as procedural justice, and incorporated them in their work, or consciously been on the lookout for signs of injustice and implicit bias.

An example of what the Flint Water Advisory Task Force called "callous and dismissive responses to the citizens' expressed concerns" [264] includes:

---

[260] Hearing 3, Section 2, at 16:40
[261] Hearing 3, Section 1, at 40:10.
[262] Hearing 3, Section 2, at 5:25.
[263] Hearing 3, Section 1, at 1:13:55
[264] Flint Water Advisory Task Force Report at p. 2.

"We sat here and argued. I said our water's poisoned, they said no it's not, you're fine. ... I've never been talked to like I've been so ignorant or stupid."[265]

This sort of response contributed to what the Advisory Task Force's finding that "MDEQ, specifically its [Office of Drinking Water and Municipal Assistance], suffers from cultural shortcomings that prevent it from adequately serving and protecting the public health of Michigan residents."[266] These "cultural shortcomings" are precisely the sort of thing the 2009 and 2010 Environmental Justice Plans would have been addressed by training employees and integrating environmental justice principles into their work responsibilities.

Some witnesses, like Professor Mohai, believed that while "the 2009 draft had some teeth in it . . . the 2010 version was really the result of pulling all the teeth out of the 2009 version." They agreed with Mohai's conclusion, "I don't think the 2010 version would have done anything."[267] However, we also heard testimony from others, like Professor Gosman, who feel differently.

Professor Gosman argued that requirements for training and the integration of environmental justice principles into DEQ operations were still in the 2010 plan. "[T]hings like operationalizing environmental justice into strategic planning, training staff to think about environmental justice issues, prioritizing responses to community complaints in environmental justice areas, these things I think do matter." "If you take them seriously as an agency, they do affect your decision making."[268] She then added that "I think that awareness was a huge piece that was missing in this problem. People were not thinking about it from an environmental justice perspective, they were thinking about it from an economic perspective."

This led Professor Gosman to conclude that: "If [the 2010 plan] had been implemented in a serious way, and that whole piece of it had really been put into, integrated into, the DEQ, I think that would have made . . . could have made a difference."[269] We agree.

3. Procedural justice and administrative processes.

The Commission's concern here is straightforward. Procedural environmental justice does not simply require inviting people to public hearings, it requires that people be provided with *meaningful* opportunities to participate. The Commission applauds the significant strides made by DEQ and other state agencies in providing *more* opportunity for input, often offering

---

[265] Melissa Mays, Flint resident, Hearing 3, session 4 at 39:58.
[266] *Id.* at p. 28.
[267] Hearing 3, Section 1, at 13:32:30.
[268] Hearing 3, Section 2, at 42:50.
[269] *Id.* at 45:00

multiple hearings covering different days and times of day. But *more* is not enough, and hearings are not *meaningful* if the public lacks the ability to offer potentially effective testimony.

Government decisions that involve issues affecting environment and public health are based on the best science available. They are made by people, often scientists, engineers, or doctors,  who have extensive training in their individual areas of expertise. These experts know what information they require to make informed science-based decisions, and they define the information using terms like "particulates," "carcinogens," "spatial averaging zone," and "benchmark ambient concentrations." They measure in units like micrograms (µg) and micrograms per cubic meter (µg/m³), and use things like the Empirical Kinetic Modeling Approach to determine pertinent and essential details like an "annual arithmetic mean" or the very different "annual geometric mean."

On the other hand, people who are entitled to have a meaningful opportunity for input into those same decisions use terms like "gunk" and "gooey stuff" to describe what they find on their windows. They talk about "putrid odors" and "teary eyes" to describe the air they breathe. And, in the case of the Flint Water Crisis they use words like "brown," "cloudy," "stinky" or "awful tasting" to describe their water.

We heard testimony that Flint residents believed there were no mechanisms to ensure they could be heard, that there was no way they were going to be listened to. For example:

> "In my interviews with community members in Flint, they told me there were no mechanisms available to have their concerns heard. There was no way they were going to be listened to."[270]

How is a person who doesn't know the difference between a hydrocarbon and a hydrofluorocarbon supposed to know whether the aerodynamic diameter of the "gunk" suspended in their ambient air is made up of particulates in the PM10 or PM2.5 scale? If the public is to have meaningful participation, they need to be provided with the equivalent of a foreign language interpreter.

This person would need, depending on the issue at hand, to be a fully trained scientist, engineer and/or doctor whose responsibility is to learn people's concerns and advocate on their behalf.

---

[270] Michael Mascarenhas, Hearing 3, section 1 at 41:00.

F. Corrective Justice:

As stated earlier, the Michigan Civil Rights Commission finds Kuehn's third principle, corrective justice, to be essential. As illustrated in our examination of housing discrimination in Flint, the failure to repair the harm suffered by discrimination is itself ongoing discrimination that causes ongoing harm. The financial losses of Flint residents, whether in property value, expenses incurred as a result of the water contamination, ongoing medical expenses, or otherwise, are not simply one-time events. A failure to secure a remedy that properly compensates them now will result in their continuing to suffer the effects for the rest of their lives.

This Commission believes corrective justice is a critical part of environmental justice. It finds that the Flint Water Crisis requires fairness in identifying and punishing those responsible. The Commission further finds that environmental justice requires that those harmed by the water contamination be treated fairly by remedying the water infrastructure problems, and restoring and/or compensating them appropriately.

Again, however, the Commission also recognizes the legal authority of the Attorney General's office to investigate, bring criminal charges and secure punishments for law breaking. Properly addressing the damages inflicted on individuals and communities is better handled through the civil and criminal actions being taken by the Attorney General on behalf of the State and the City of Flint, and by the civil litigation brought by attorneys on behalf of Flint residents and others affected.

The Commission neither seeks to impede these efforts nor duplicate them. Therefore, we will not address the environmental justice principle of corrective justice other than to state that it is required in this instance. We will, however, continue to monitor the progress of such efforts and will address them when appropriate.

IV. EMERGENCY MANAGEMENT AND SYSTEMIC RACISM AT PLAY

The current emergency manager (EM) law has both proponents and opponents. State government has traditionally developed many policies affecting state-local relations, from debt limit to auditing requirements, and including state takeover of municipalities in financial distress.

We focus our attention on determining if and how the EM law addresses the role of space and race in Michigan and how that serves to counter the production and reproduction of spatial and structural racism as evidenced in communities like Flint.

If you live in Michigan, there is a 10% chance that you have lived under emergency management since 2009. But if you are a black Michigander, the odds are 50/50.[271]

Whether one supports or opposes the EM law is not the issue. What is clear is that its application in Michigan has had a racially disparate effect. The record reveals that communities of color have been starkly overrepresented in jurisdictions placed under emergency management. This does not mean that the law or the people administering it are racist in their decisions to appoint an emergency manager.

We believe "fixing" the emergency manager law is not the proper place to start. Before we look for better ways to fix the problems associated with the EM law, we must ask whether we have properly identified the problems.

If a local jurisdiction's problem is really poor bookkeeping or bad money management, the EM law might be an effective tool. But poor bookkeeping does not explain the overrepresentation of people of color in decaying urban areas surrounded by greater wealth. The problems that created the fiscal emergency are generally broader than balancing the books, and if it is going to work, the solution must be as well.

Using the EM law to balance the books by slashing the budget not only fails to address most of the root causes of the financial distress, it exacerbates existing gaps between urban and suburban communities, and erects additional barriers to narrowing the racial gap. In short, the EM law as applied far too often addresses the problems of already financially stricken governments in second class communities, segregated based on race, wealth and opportunity, by appointing an emergency manager whose toolbox is filled with short term solutions that are

---

[271] 9.7% of all Michiganders, 49.8%. See e.g., Richard C. Sadler and Andrew R. Highsmith, "Rethinking Tiebout: The Contribution of Political Fragmentation and Racial/Economic Segregation to the Flint Water Crisis," *Environmental Justice*, (2016) at 7.   (NEED FULL CITE)

contrary to the long term interests of the people living there. This Commission examined the relationship between the City of Flint and its suburbs and found the following:

1. Declining property values in Flint continue to erode the property tax revenues for Flint.

2. Strong historical racial division between Flint and its suburbs and a lack of cooperation to address problems they created together.

3. Eroding business and industrial base leading to declining jobs in Flint while growth or no decline in the suburbs.

4. Continual flight of whites from Flint to the suburbs.

5. Declining income tax base as a source of revenue for Flint.

6. A history of spatial race discrimination, the legacy of which contributed greatly to the city's decline and the decline's disparate effects on people of color.

7. An aging and oversized water system that has been left to those least able to pay the highest water bills in the country.

Each of these has played a role in creating Flint's financial emergencies, yet none are addressed by the current EM law. Given the foregoing, how can a community like Flint increase its revenue base? And how can the state through an EM assist a community, such as Flint, address its financial distress, on both a short-term and long-term basis? Because the current EM law does nothing to address the foregoing factors, it is a fatally flawed response to the challenges facing Flint.

As a state, and as a nation, we must face the role race played in creating the urban problems and economic disparities that confront us. The Flint Water Crisis is the product of over 75 years in the making. Some form of emergency management may be necessary from time to time, but we will not cure the disease if we only treat one symptom.

We heard testimony from witnesses that the structure of the current EM law is too narrow, and that balancing the books and leaving does nothing if expenses still exceed revenues.

> That's the problem, that the state statute does not address the long term stability and economic climate for the community. The emergency manager goal is to balance the books, and if you can try to get something else done, I guess

you can try that. But that's not what you go there for. And then the state's idea is to get out as soon as possible.[272]

The state must make one of the duties of an emergency manager the restructuring of an economy in that city for economic stability and must support with the finances to do it.[273]

We agree.

Presently the biggest difference between a local government official and an emergency manager is that the emergency manager does not have the residents' interests as its first priority. Balancing the books alone is at least as much about the welfare of creditors and other outside interests, as it is about the residents. Investing to build a better future is not part of an emergency manager's job, but it should be. A more comprehensive approach to addressing communities facing financial distress is required than is currently found in the EM law.

The Commission also notes that the current emergency manager law imposes a policy prescription that may even create "insolvent cities" or "minimal cities" which could result from the imposition of dramatic austerity measures. Examples of such measures include budget cuts and asset sales leaving a stripped down version of core services functions like irregular police and fire protection or rudimentary sanitation and water supplies. These can render communities like Flint barely operable, unable to meet obligations to creditors or address the needs of its residents. The fear is that such measures could create what the Kerner Report described as the creation of two societies, separate and unequal, black and white. We must prevent this from occurring.

The Commission heard of instances when emergency managers came in and took over positions, corrected problems and created efficiencies that made a positive difference. However, they left without training or preparing the people who would take over these responsibilities, sometimes the very people who had them before. Thus, any positive progress that was made was lost with the departure of the EM.

Eric Lupher likened this to the Bible parable that if you give a man a fish he eats for a day, but if you teach him to fish he eats for a lifetime. Cities that came out of emergency management only to "recycle," he said, did so "because the municipal employees that were there didn't learn to fish. ... They don't have the

---

[272] Michael Stampfler, former Emergency manager for Pontiac with nearly 30 years of city management experience, hearing 3, session 3 at 1:11:24.
[273] *Id.* at 1:13:08

financial management tools, they don't have the inventory controls, they don't have the basic management skills to run a government."[274]

We agree. An important part of an emergency manager's task must be to ensure their success is sustainable by the staff in place when they leave.

We heard testimony about emergency managers succeeding by using powers granted to them, but that are unavailable to local elected officials. Former Benton Harbor Emergency Manager Joe Harris, for example, spoke of the ability to renegotiate union contracts.[275]

We believe this creates an appearance of bias which can and should be prevented. The current emergency manager law assumes that there is a need for BOTH special powers and an outside person. Why is it assumed that the existing political structure could not fix things if it had the special powers? Why is it assumed that an outsider could not fix things without special powers? It MAY be the case that both are necessary, but this should require two separate findings.

The Commission heard testimony indicating that some of the problems in Flint would best be addressed regionally, but that there was no mechanism in place or authority to do so.

Chris Kolb, who co-chaired the Governor's Flint Water Advisory Task Force, questioned:

> In a state, and in a region, where we had excess water capacity, why did we think we needed more? And when we are making decisions on infrastructure that cost billions of dollars, we should be able to, in this state, make decisions that take that into account.[276]

He later answered his own question, saying: "There is no system in Michigan really for regionalism . . . That really for us was the problem."[277]

This Commission believes that Michigan's strong home rule cities can sometimes work against each other's interests, thereby creating challenges that may best be solved if approached on a regional basis. Viewing Flint in isolation without considering its relationships with the suburbs is short sighted. A much broader approach is required to address problems that were created by regional policies or practices. Fostering regional cooperation to solve problems may, in fact, be the most appropriate reason for appointing an emergency manager. If an emergency manager is given powers beyond those of Flint's elected officials, they should also be given the ability to

---

[274] Hearing 3, session 3 at 1:16:14.
[275] Hearing 3, session 3 at 49:00.
[276] Hearing 3, session 2 at 1:18:40.
[277] Id. at 1:19:20

reach beyond Flint's borders if that is where the solution, and perhaps even the cause, can be found.

Most glaringly, we heard from numerous Flint residents that they are no longer heard when an emergency manager is in place.

We have been under siege for two years. And for well over a year we were screaming, and nobody listened.[278]

I drove people to Lansing on a regular basis, way before it even came out in the media, we were crying about this water.[279]

The people of Michigan voted down the emergency manager law on Monday, the following Wednesday they had another one, that we couldn't vote down. Do we trust the Government? NO![280]

And all of these people out here, they stood outside and told city hall, the water is bad, it's discolored, its repulsive, it smells.[281]

This is never acceptable. Every resident has the right to be heard by the elected officials making decisions that affect the resident's life and health. This becomes even more important when an emergency manager is appointed to oversee local governments in distress. A manager from outside the community does not share the community's interests, and may not even understand them or know what they are. It is therefore imperative that (s)he listens to them. But this is not enough; the key is to ensure meaningful involvement by hearing from local residents. We believe that local residents should have meaningful input into the decisions that affect them.

---

[278] Valerie Soughall, Flint resident, hearing 1 at 1:15:48.
[279] Sister Janice Mohammed, Flint resident, Hearing 1 at 1:39:11.
[280] Paul Herring, Sr., Flint resident, hearing 1 at 1:41:30.
[281] Carolyn Shannon, Flint resident, hearing 3, session 4 at 1:09:50.

V.   CONCLUSION

We end where we started – with a number of key concepts: Implicit bias and systemic racism. Both teach us that race will affect the decisions we make, unless we consciously undertake to address these shortcomings.

Housing, education, the environment, and emergency management. Each is connected to the other, and any policy that affects one, affects the others. Drawing a clear policy line defining where one ends and the next begins is impossible.

The same is true of racism, racialization, and systemic racism. They overlap and it is usually impossible to define precisely which applies and caused a particular outcome to be racially disparate. The structure, norms, policies and practices cut across institutions, neighborhoods, and communities with cumulative and compound effects. This Commission believes that, particularly applied to government, getting too caught up in precisely defining which is at play is both distracting and counterproductive. When we know policy will bring about disparate outcomes based on the color of people's skin, it is our responsibility to do address it. It is not enough to say the result is unintended.

The manifestation of the Flint Water Crisis may or may not have involved bad actors, race-based decisions, criminal neglect, government negligence, or simply a lack of empathy for "the other." That will be determined by others. But to mitigate against or even prevent crises like this one we must look deeper.

It is abundantly clear that race played a major role in developing the policies and causing the events that turned Flint into a decaying and largely abandoned urban center, a place where a crisis like this one was all but inevitable. We cannot predict what the next crisis will be, when it will occur, or in which decaying urban center it will happen. But we do know that unless we do something, it will occur, and it will disparately harm people of color.

So was the Flint Water Crisis a case of discrimination?

The answer depends in large part with how "discrimination" is defined. Discrimination in the legal sense is defined and limited by our civil rights laws. In this context the question is whether an action is legal or illegal. In a more generalized use, "discrimination" also includes acts that do not meet the technical legal requirements. In this larger context the question is closer to whether the action was fair or unfair. Such an answer tells us not just about who we exclude versus include, but about the very foundation and ethos of our society, our moral fabric, our identity.

Ultimately the legal question of whether the Flint Water Crisis was the result of illegal discrimination is one that is left to the courts to decide. We do not seek to interfere with those proceedings, and therefore will not answer the legal question directly.

We can say that those pursuing civil rights claims will face an uphill climb.

There is no legal redress available to children who grew up in Flint because their father or grandfather returned from fighting for other's freedom in World War II were denied the ability to purchase a home because the G.I. bill and Federal Housing Authority effectively excluded black neighborhoods. It is indisputable that African Americans were routinely discriminated against by conduct that was legal at the time and thus was not illegal discrimination. And even if it had been illegal at the time, the time in which to have filed a discrimination case has long since passed. As such, although we find that the history of housing in Flint is replete with spatial racism, racially discriminatory loan and realty practices, racialized structure, structural and systemic racism, any such legal claim not based on recent events does not rise to the level of a legal claim

We leave open the door to the possibility that a complaint may be brought to us that will meet the necessary legal requirements and falls within our jurisdiction. We note that the strongest argument for such a case would likely be a disparate impact claim under federal housing law based upon the 2015 U.S. Supreme Court decision, _Texas Department of Housing & Community Affairs v. The Inclusive Communities Project, Inc._[282] However, it is our understanding that the Department of Housing and Urban Development ("HUD"), who would be the most appropriate agency to pursue such a case under this federal law theory, has to date also not found a sufficient basis for doing so in this instance.

Nothing in this report should be read to imply that we do or do not believe there is merit in any of the civil suits that have been or may be brought related to the Flint Water Crisis. We have not reviewed the cases in detail and have not considered the issues presented by claims on theories and laws other than the ones discussed here. However, we note that while some testimony suggested that various manufacturers were responsible for the pollution that made the Flint River unusable, the choice to switch away from the Flint River as a water source was made because the river lacked a sufficient quantity of water, not quality. (_See_ p. 42.) Additionally, the Flint River water intake was upstream from the industrial polluters, and any quality issues related to the river water have had more to do with farm fertilizer and road salt run off than industrial pollution.

The Attorney General's Office has brought criminal charges related to the Flint Water Crisis, and indicates more may be coming. Those charged are innocent until proven guilty, but the charges do indicate that the Attorney General believes that some of the people involved in the events surrounding this crisis acted with some degree of _mens rea_ (criminal intent). We have not considered criminal liability in this report.

There is no single cause for a crisis like the one still occurring in Flint; it requires a perfect storm of causes. Pointing the finger at any one specific cause for this crisis does not diminish the fact

---

[282] Citation

that the legacy of past policies in areas like housing, employment, the tax base and regionalization are all interconnected to the present. Identifying one bad actor doesn't indicate there aren't others.

Nor does it matter that people of color are not the only victims. Race, racism, structural racialization and systemic racism were responsible for the policies and events that created white flight, which decreased property values in the city while increased them in the suburbs, and trapped anyone who remained in Flint regardless of color.

We find even the argument over whether a disparate impact results from policies and practices based on socioeconomics or racial differences to be more semantic than substantive. We have seen how a history of racist or racialized policies and practices resulted in African Americans being deprived of building wealth and taking advantage of opportunities.

The contamination of Flint's water system is deplorable, but it is only a symptom of a much larger disease, one that poisons all our structures and systems. Racialized outcomes do not need to be intentional. The poison of systemic racism will produce and reproduce them unless we consciously address then through implementation of policies and practices that have a racial equity framework. This is true of our government and it is true of ourselves.

The conditions that allowed the Flint Water Crisis are rooted in a time when racial separation and discrimination was intentional and expressed. A time when racism was not only accepted, it was official government policy but continued as accepted practices, processes, norms and rituals even when such policies were no longer official. Systemically we continue to produce racially disparate harm and benefit.

The fact that the problem is systemic and may be unintentional is an explanation, not an excuse. We can either consciously do something about it, or intentionally ignore it. That the problem is systemic doesn't mean there is nobody to blame, we are all to blame.

"...being colorblind is not the solution, it is the problem."

We must recognize that being colorblind is not the solution, it is the problem. Implicit bias and systemic racism ensure that when we refuse to see color, we are actually allowing it to influence our decisions while reinforcing racialized outcomes. Perpetuating those results without attempting to remedy past harm, and without consciously ensuring we don't cause new harm, isn't colorblindness, it is racism.

VI.   RECOMMENDATIONS

Our recommendations seek to take a comprehensive approach to understand why our system creates and recreates spatial separation of wealth and opportunity largely along racial lines. Studies are replete with examples of racially disparate outcomes when it comes to education, employment, business, housing, and health.

Accordingly, we take a deliberate and inclusive approach moving beyond our comfort zone. In this regard we offer the following recommendations:

1. **The Michigan Civil Rights Commission and the Michigan Department of Civil Rights must do a better job of listening to the constituencies we represent and of making their priorities, our priorities.**

Before we make recommendations to others, we must first take an honest look at ourselves. How did we (both the Commission and the Department) respond to this crisis? While we believe we have responded and performed appropriately since the emergency was formally declared, we did not do all we could and should have done prior to that time.

We do not intend to offer excuses (there are none) or explanations for our failure to act sooner. We will not try to determine with the advantage of hindsight exactly what we could or should have done. What we will do, what we must do, is acknowledge that in the earlier stages of this crisis the people of Flint were calling out for help and regretfully we did not answer the call.

Flint residents began objecting to using the Flint River as a water source even before the switch was made. The objections intensified after the change – when the water being delivered to people's kitchens turned color, smelled awful and tasted repugnant. People took to the streets, petitioned government offices, and appeared in nearly every newspaper, television, radio, and online news source in the state.

It does not matter whether we failed to act because we concluded that, because there were also white victims race was not playing a role, because we saw the crisis only in economic terms, or because we saw water quality as a scientific issue only. In fact, even if we failed to act because we never heard about the protests in Flint, it would only expose our lack of awareness of an issue that was vitally important to one of the constituencies we are supposed to protect.

We cannot say that the outcome would have changed had we done what we now believe we should have. We will never know. What we do know is that had we done our job, the people of Flint would have known SOMEONE was listening to them, and fighting for them. That alone would have been a significant change.

We could have done more sooner, we should have done so, we did not. Our first recommendations are therefore to ourselves. Additionally, as we hope others reading this will do, we commit ourselves to making the changes recommended.

a. **The Department will develop a mechanism for Department staff to identify and inform the Commission of instances in which the civil rights of a community or constituency are being ignored.**

The primary responsibility of both the Department and Commission is the investigation of complaints brought by individuals and/or which relate to specific conduct by an identified individual or entity. We have also been involved with issues that have statewide implications. The Flint Water Crisis tells us that we have not enough to proactively identify more localized issues that are the priority of one or more of our constituent communities. We certainly will not be able to address them all, but we should be reviewing our complaints for trends and issues that have broader implications.

The Department has outreach staff that are active in many communities on an ongoing basis, and others who traverse the state to give presentations on civil rights issues. The Department will direct these staff members to regularly inquire of, or survey, those they with whom they interface to identify issues that their community currently sees as significant. This information will be presented to the Commission as determined by the Director.

b. **The Commission will relocate scheduled meetings to affected communities when appropriate.**

The Commission schedules meeting dates at the beginning the year, but locations are selected over the course of the year. The Commission will use the information provided by the Department to identify concerns and locate meetings in those communities. Concerned members of the public will be invited to address the Commission either during an extended public comment period, or a separate hearing.

The Commission may also ask the Department to hold hearings for this purpose on dates when the Commission may not be meeting.

c. **The Department and Commission will facilitate communication of concerns even when not adopting them as a priority of their own.**

Though unable to become actively involved in every issue, the Commission and Department must recognize that we are the voice (sometimes the only voice) for underserved and vulnerable communities who may lack direct access to government. Thus, even when we are not able to fully adopt such concerns as our own, going forward we will share such concerns that come to us with other government agencies and officials as appropriate.

2. **Develop a deeper understanding of the roles of structural racialization and implicit bias, and how they affect decision making throughout all branches of State Government and specifically within all the state departments.**

   a. **The Governor's Office should invite experts on the cognitive psychology and neuroscience of implicit bias to provide training to the Cabinet and Mission Flint Action Team and require all state departments, including DEQ and DHHS, to do the same for their staff.**

   Unconscious bias is real, it is neurologically driven, it is unavoidable, and without exception every one of us has it. These unconscious biases are created and reinforced by media messages and dominant social narratives about history, politics, power and the economy. By definition, this means that we must be conscious of race if we are to avoid making decisions that are influenced by it. Never stopping to challenge ourselves about whether our unconscious biases are directing our actions means we are accepting that they will do so.

   b. **Government at all levels must gain and encourage a better understanding of structural racialization and the role it plays in perpetuating disparate outcomes.**

   Pretending we do not see color or race is denying neurological reality – and it is a "privilege" available only to those of us who are white. Structural racialization consists of the inter-institutional dynamics that produce and reproduce racially disparate outcomes over time without regard to intent. These racially desperate outcomes occur in areas of health, education, income, transportation, housing, and the environment as evidenced in Flint. Historically, these forces served to perpetuate notions of white supremacy most evident in institutions of slavery and Jim Crow segregation. Today, these same forces continue in different institutional forms to protect and reinforce notions of white privilege. The oppressive and hierarchical nature of these forces, however, remain the same.

   Segregation of space plays an important role in understanding structural racialization as demonstrated in the separation of Flint from the remainder of Genesee County. In this context, we need to be more aware of the spatialization of race and the racialization of space throughout Michigan. Flint is an example of the disparity in income, wealth creation, health, and access to public services when compared to communities located outside of Flint and yet located within Genesee County.

c. **Government must recognize that an unfair advantage cannot be corrected simply by refraining from being unfair in the future; policies must be adopted to counteract the continuing harm caused by past racism.**

Local, State and Federal governments were actively involved in providing housing opportunities to some and denying them to others. Public and private actions combined to instantly lower the resale value of property after it was purchased by African Americans, while creating conditions where future generations would benefit from the purchases by white Americans. Generations of students were denied equal educational opportunities.

Certainly there are programs and policies today that disadvantage all the poor, or all persons living in decaying urban areas, regardless of their race. However, it is not mere coincidence that these same policies universally have a disparate negative impact on persons of color. Government's failure to do anything to correct the disparity that it helped to create means it continues to perpetuate harms caused by its past racism. Prime examples in Flint were the Floral Park and St. John communities where the use of urban renewal and highway programs destroyed mostly these black-occupied communities.

3. **Provide environmental justice to all people in Michigan.**

As discussed earlier, the role of environmental justice in the case of Flint is critically important. The Governor's Task Force Report recognized it and found the existence of environmental injustice in the disparate outcomes faced by Flint residents and the lack of meaningful participation by residents in their government. Testimony received during our hearings bore this out.

a. **Write and legislatively adopt a robust environmental justice plan that provides (1) meaningful public (community) participation, (2) integration of governmental decision-making, (3) interagency cooperation, and (4) a means for the public to request responsive state action, i.e., to appeal certain decisions.**

In the past, great effort was expended to develop an environmental justice plan for Michigan. Had the 2009 Environmental Justice Plan been adopted and implemented, it may have made the Flint Water Crisis much less likely. The petition process in the 2009 Plan would have allowed Flint residents to elevate their concerns by filing a petition with the Interdepartmental Working Group. Because the Interdepartmental Working Group (IWG) would have included directors of the DEQ and the Department of Health and Human Services as well as the Governor's environmental policy advisor, there would have been recognition at the highest levels of the problems in Flint. And if the IWG accepted the petition, there would have been an action plan to address the problems. We also recommend that the IWG be expanded to include the Director of the Department of Civil Rights and Michigan's Chief Medical Officer (currently housed in DHHS).

b. **A major component of environmental justice is community participation in decision-making – therefore, Michigan's emergency manager law must be amended to provide for local representation and the possibility to appeal an adverse decision.**

One of the key principles of environmental justice is that those who will be affected by decisions must be a part of the decision-making process. While emergency manager laws are addressed elsewhere, it must be recognized here that the Michigan's EM laws, and in particular their application with respect to the city of Flint, are irreconcilably contradictory.

c. **Acknowledge the cumulative effect of environmental hazards, and make cumulative effect part of the official decision-making process.**

The difficulty of quantifying the cumulative effect of environmental hazards is insufficient reason to ignore the fact that the same level of a potentially harmful pollutant will cause greater harm to persons with existing health problems and/or who are already being exposed to numerous other potentially harmful pollutants. The cumulative effect of multiple pollutants must be considered in determining what amounts of each pollutant is permissible.

d. **Require a more holistic review of the cost benefit analysis conducted when assessing and placing potential environmental hazards.**

We recognize that some level of environmental risk and/or harm may be offset by necessity. We also recognize that one must consider whether minimizing potentially harmful emissions may be so costly that it would prevent the availability of something that serves the public interest. It is completely reasonable to conclude that refining oil into gasoline is necessary even though there will be some environmental cost. That said, we must then separate the question of location of such hazards from the question of who will benefit. If the risks are deemed to be in everyone's interests, they should be shouldered equally be everyone. Placing multiple hazards in one community and none in another is the privilege of the powerful, but it is not environmental justice. It is particularly unjust when those who reap the greatest benefits also bear the least risk of harm.

4. Replace or restructure Michigan's emergency manager law.

The Commission understands that some sort of State-imposed emergency powers may be necessary when a community faces a fiscal emergency that it is unable to address on its own. However, the present emergency manager law is flawed in a number of ways that violate the principle of representative government, and which ignore the very purpose for the law.

a. A law intended to help a community recover from a fiscal emergency must also focus on solving the problem that caused the emergency, thereby returning the community to sustainable fiscal health.

Testimony presented to this Commission described an emergency manager law that is directed only at the short term goal of balancing a community's books, without consideration for how doing so will affect the community's longer term financial stability. The types of severe budget cuts and asset disposal that result too often have the effect of actually worsening the community's long term economic stability. New revenue sources cannot be developed by a community if it is unable to attract either new businesses or residents.

In her article, "The New Minimal Cities,"[283] Stanford Law Professor Michelle Wilde Anderson explored the consequences of municipalities facing household poverty, loss of population and physical deterioration, ending up in some form of bankruptcy or state receivership. In cutting costs and diverting revenues to debt payments, cities like Flint have taken dramatic austerity measures. She raises an important question: "Is there a point where the city should no longer cut public services and sell public assets, even in the face of unmet obligations to creditors? If so, what is that point?" Professor Anderson focuses on the interests of

---

[283] Michelle W. Anderson, _The New Minimal Cities_, 123 Yale Law Journal 1118 (2014).

residents who live in cities, like Flint, and are affected by such cuts. Effective tools are necessary to manage the decline and allow local units of government, like Flint, to effectively manage the decline and rebuild across economic cycles. Michigan's current EM structure fails to address these issues.

Michigan's present EM structure temporarily replaces city decision makers and managers and with others who are believed to have better experience, training and skills. However, once the community's books are in balance, the former leadership frequently returns without the training required to reach the expertise of those acting in the interim. Part of the role of any emergency usurpation of local power must be to prepare the local government to effectively manage and govern communities like Flint.

b. **Provide emergency managers with regional authority; not all solutions are local because not all problems are local.**

This recommendation is explored further below, but is critical in the emergency manager context. Part of the problem with the Flint water system is that the infrastructure was built for a community of 200,000 residents plus substantial commercial industry, over half of which have relocated to the suburbs. Flint residential water rates are high in large part because the system is so oversized and deteriorated that the city must pump two gallons for every one that ultimately reaches a consumer. Fiscal crises like the one resulting in an emergency manager for Flint have their roots in suburban governments and people that took advantage of a city's resources and then left the city to deal with the consequences. When the state appoints an emergency manager to address a fiscal problem that is not being addressed by the people who created it, that emergency power should extend to those who are unwilling to take responsibility.

c. **Bifurcate the process of naming an emergency manager and providing special authority or powers.**

The present emergency manager law replaces local control, but also provides the replacing manager with special powers that local government did not have. This appears to be based upon an illogical assumption that, while the outside manager cannot succeed without the special powers, local government could not succeed even with them.

An unelected appointee should not be brought in if there is a capable elected mayor to give the needed authority to, and special authority should not be given to an appointee automatically. Both steps may be necessary, but the necessity needs to be established separately, not assumed.

d. **A declaration of a fiscal emergency that requires emergency management or other state usurpation of local government powers, must include a statement that analyzes the root cause of the emergency and outlines how it will be addressed.**

Simply recognizing the existence of an emergency should not be a basis for replacing local representative government control. The process must begin by establishing what caused the fiscal emergency, and then determining how it can be addressed. Emergency management cannot be a one-size-fits-all solution. It must in each instance be tailored to address the cause and not only the emergency itself.

e. **Locally elected representative government must continue to play some role, and an emergency manager must have direct accountability to an elected official (the Governor).**

The Commission recommends that whatever the replacement for the current emergency manager law is, it needs to include a process for appealing significant EM decisions. One option would be to allow a majority of an existing elected council to appeal a decision to the Governor. While this may not ultimately change many of an emergency manager's decisions, it would increase the level of attention a challenged matter receives. A decision would not only more likely to receive careful reflection by the emergency manager who made it, it would more likely draw media attention. Even more important, it would make the Governor accountable, something that would add an element of caution to big decisions.

5. **Acknowledge the role race and racism have played in our history, and how it continues to impact our present, in order to adopt policies that consider and address it.**

   a. **Reject the idea that our society has or should become "colorblind", which perpetuates the status quo by ignoring or overlooking the impact of decisions made within a racialized system, as well as the implicit biases that assert themselves if we do not consciously recognize them.**

   In both the private and public spheres, the concepts of equality and colorblindness have been falsely equated. This has been deliberate and/or strategic in many instances, colorblindness has also been benignly pursued by those who want to believe in the myth that it represents. Because our subconscious brain function makes it impossible to actually be colorblind, pretending or fooling ourselves into believing that we are colorblind means accepting and acting on our perceptions of color. Perhaps even more contradictory is that collectively and intentionally acting without recognizing color AFTER having previously done the opposite strategically rewards the very conduct the concept of colorblindness now recognizes as evil.

According to Eduardo Bonilla-Silva, a sociology professor at Duke University colorblindness represents modern-day bigotry or the common manifestation of the "new racism". In his book, *White Supremacy and Racism in the Post-Civil Rights Era*, Bonilla-Silva argues that racism has become more subtle since the end of segregation. Professor Bonilla-Silva argues that the whites view the 1960s as the end of racism, but in truth, the events of the 1960s and 70s produced an alteration of the order.

That alteration upended the rhetoric of the civil rights struggle, Bonilla-Silva said, so that historically oppressed groups would seem to be the perpetrators of discrimination, not its victims. An example is Rev. Martin Luther King, Jr.'s quote from the 1963 March on Washington where he stated "I believe that people should be judged by the content of their character." However, people then eliminate the history and contemporary practice of discrimination while playing the morality tale.

The well-intentioned argument in favor of colorblindness is that it is unjust to allow considerations of color to seep into public policy or personal decision-making. However, we have seen in Flint that past public policy had profoundly discriminatory results. It can be argued that the prior policies were themselves colorblind, but this line of thinking simply proves the fallacy of the concept that colorblindness is a good thing.

In an individual, "colorblindness" may or may not be well intended. Until a person recognizes that (like everyone else) they have unconscious or implicit biases, they may well believe otherwise. However, once a person becomes aware of the universality of implicit biases, continuing to pretend to be "colorblind" is strategic racism.

In public policy, the reality of past racism is that its harm is as every bit as persistent as its existence is undisputable. If enacting legislation that that will perpetuate the harm caused by past racism, or that will have a disparately negative affect on people of color, is considered "colorblind" – "colorblind" legislation is strategic racism.

6. **Rebuild Trust and Credibility:**

   a. **Create a "Truth and Reconciliation Commission."**

The City of Flint and the residents have faced numerous challenges arising from the uncovering of toxic lead in the drinking water. A few examples include dependency on bottled water for the basic daily necessities of life, health related problems and government repeated failure to hear the voices of the residents. A common theme heard from the residents was the loss of trust they have in government and others. To build a viable and vibrant community there is a need for mutual trust between residents and government. In order for Flint's municipal water supply to remain sustainable, public trust must be rebuilt between residents and regulatory agencies. Without it recovery and long-term sustainable efforts will be hampered and face possible derailment. Mayor Weaver at the January 11th Flint Water Town Hall admitted, "we sure don't trust." Amen!!

The Commission recommends the development and formation of a Truth and Reconciliation Commission, following a two-step process: (1) a Convening Panel to be properly assembled and trained, and (2) the Convening Panel to be vested with writing a mandate and charge for a Truth and Reconciliation Commission, and then interview and select commissioners.

We recognize that examples of successful "truth and reconciliation commissions" in the U.S. is virtually impossible to find. However, this does not mean that Flint cannot be a guiding example of what such a commission could accomplish. In the few cases we have found, one hallmark of successful Truth and Reconciliation Commissions (TRC) has been the inclusion of a convening panel, composed of residents who, by the nature of their role in households and small community groups, are well trusted within the community. A "council of elders" model for creating a convening panel has been studied and implemented successfully in First Nations TRC processes. By deliberately inserting a mechanism for involving trusted community members in the selection of commissioners, residents are more likely to be engaged in the Truth and Reconciliation Commission process with meaningful involvement and power in the decision making process.

The Convening Panel should be provided with resources regarding the creation of TRC-type commissions and the role of similar commissions in rebuilding trust within communities. Following a prescribed timeline, the Convening Panel would prepare a mandate for a Truth and Reconciliation Commission, create an interview process, and select the Commissioners. One approach would be for the Truth and Reconciliation Commission to be accountable to the Convening Panel throughout the process, and through this Panel, to the residents of Flint. The final product of the Truth and Reconciliation Commission would be a report, written for the residents of Flint, and delivered to the Convening Panel. This report would serve to increase the community voice and address specific concerns identified by residents.

We recognize that trust is built over time by following through with the promises one makes. Likewise, credibility — the quality or power of inspiring belief — grows in much the same way. The principles of trust and credibility are tightly linked and build on each other. In the case of Flint, we recognize this process will take time and will be painfully slow.

In the case of the Flint Water Crisis, the Commission recognizes that at all level of government there was a failure to listen to the voices of the residents and safeguard the residents. Likewise, others, whether in business, philanthropy, or government also failed to speak up and act. Residents have been harmed and their faith in government and other institutions deeply shaken and in many cases, lost. But it is time to begin finding ways to rebuild the trust and credibility to grow and rebuild the great City of Flint. We recommend that the leaders of Flint will take up this recommendation and charge forward.

In creating a Convening Panel, we believe there are civic and community leaders from different parts of Flint and Genesee County who have the standing and respect in the community to help move this process forward. The creation of a convening panel can serve as an important stepping stone towards creating a "Truth and Reconciliation Commission" that can play in revitalizing the community.

b. Build a Racial Equity Framework.

To minimize the risk of another Flint Water Crisis, we must pledge to eliminate racial inequities in our communities. This means developing a "collective impact" approach firmly grounded in inclusion and equity. Government, at all levels, can play a key role in fostering and building collaborations for achieving racial equity, centering community and leveraging institutional partnerships. Racial disparities are too often sustained by structures and systems that repeat patterns of exclusion. State, regional, and local governmental units have the ability to implement policy changes that can drive systemic change.

We encourage Flint, Genesee County and our State government to review different models and identify best practices, tools and resources to address racial inequities. One such initiative is GARE, Government Alliance on Race & Equity, is developing a nationwide network of governmental units focusing on these inequities. The goal is not to just eliminate the gap between whites and people of color, but to increase the success for all groups. Racial equity develops goals and outcomes that can result in improvements for all groups, but the strategies are targeted based on the needs of a particular group. Systems that are failing communities of color, are actually failing all of us. "Targeted universalism," or eliminating the gaps, increase our collective success while being cost effective in the long run.

GARE and similar initiatives and networks offer a framework for government to focus not only on individual programs, but also capacity building strategies to reduce inequities and the development and implementation of corresponding policies and programs. Examples of such strategies could include:

- **Use a racial equity framework:** Use of a racial equity framework that clearly articulates racial equity, implicit and explicit bias, and individual, institutional and structural racism.
- **Build organizational capacity:** Governmental units need to be committed to the breadth and depth of institutional transformation so that impacts are sustainable. To bring about sustainable change, our infrastructures need to be change through creating racial equity experts and teams throughout local and regional government.
- **Implement racial equity tools:** Racial inequities are not random; they have been created and sustained over time. Inequities will not disappear on their own. Tools must be used to change the policies, programs, and practices that are perpetuating inequities. New policies and programs must also be developed with a racial equity tool.
- **Be data-driven:** Measurement must take place at two levels – first, to measure the success of specific programmatic and policy changes, and second, to develop baselines, set goals and measure progress towards goals. Use of data in this manner is necessary for accountability.
- **Partner with other institutions and communities:** The work of local and regional government on racial equity is necessary, but it is not sufficient. To achieve racial equity in the community, local and regional government needs to work in partnership with communities and other institutions to achieve meaningful results.
- **Operate with urgency and accountability:** Professor John Kotter of Harvard Business School, world renowned writer on change, is often quoted in saying that to bring about change, there first must be a sense of urgency established. When change is a priority and urgency is felt, change is embraced and can take place quickly. Building in institutional accountability mechanisms via a clear plan of action will allow accountability. Collectively, we all must create greater urgency and public will to achieve racial equity.

7. **Create and implement a form of regional government (or at least regional cooperation) that would require that suburbs and the urban cores from which they grew to work collaboratively to solve problems.**

Attempts to form regional forms of government in the past 30 plus years have failed in Flint as well as other parts of the country. The results have been mixed and overall efforts at direct consolidation have proven futile. In recent years, U.S. local government entities have often formed "councils of governments", "metropolitan regional councils", or "associations of governments". These organizations serve as regional planning agencies and as forums for debating issues of regional importance, but are generally powerless relative to their individual members. Yet if there is a community in a need of a comprehensive approach to address the challenges faced, it is the City of Flint and Genesee County.

The City of Flint and Genesee County is an example of how municipal fragmentation perpetuates separate communities that are not only racially segregated but where there are clear separation of wealth and opportunity. An example was the decline in infrastructure as evidenced in Flint's water treatment plan and the appointment of an emergency manager in 2011.

The Commission supports Sadler and Highsmith's proposal (as outlined in their recent article "Rethinking Tiebout: The Contribution of Political Fragmentation and Racial/Economic Segregation to the Flint Water Crisis") to create a hybrid form of regional government referred to as "federated regionalism." Specifically, the federated regional form of government is "a regional approach that preserves political and cultural status within communities or cities, while sharing regional resources and responsibilities and balanced regional policymaking." The key is to offer a comprehensive approach where the strengths of the City of Flint combined with the resources and opportunities located in the outlining communities in Genesee County are fully leveraged. The current form of local governance in today's fast changing world is simply not working and does not address the many problems and challenges faced by certain communities.

We acknowledge that changes in the laws will be necessary and we call on government at all levels to bring about these changes. This will result in profound but necessary changes to address the inequities that currently exist in Michigan while offering a new form of government that can work to resolve the remaining imbalances in education, economic and community development, health, and transportation.

Made in the USA
Middletown, DE
17 January 2018